Catherine
TEKAKWITHA

Diego Paoletti

Catherine Tekakwitha

Copyright © 2011 Diego Paoletti

All rights reserved. No part of this publication may be reproduced, stored in a retrieval system, or transmitted in any form or by any means—electronic, mechanical, photocopy, recording, or any other—except for brief quotations in printed reviews, without prior permission from the publisher.

Printed in Canada.

ISBN-13: 978-1-77069-397-5

Preface

The two basic works on the life of Catherine Tekakwitha are from the French Jesuit missionaries Claude Chauchetiere and Pierre Cholenec. They were the only two missionaries who wrote and witnessed her death. Also, inserts have been included from their letters and collections of Catherine Tekakwitha. These letters and collections have contributed to a most complete history of what had been written of her during her life and after her death.

Catherine Tekakwitha was born in 1656 along the Mohawk River in present day United States. She died in odour of sanctity on April 17, 1680 at the Sault Saint Louis in Canada. Soon after her death, her face was suddenly transfigured to become so beautiful from the disappearance of the scars of smallpox. In 1684, Catherine Tekakwitha's relic was brought into the chapel of Saint Francis Xavier and she was the first in the Americas to be given this honour. She became known after her death from the miracles brought by her intercession.

Her Iroquois name, Tekakwitha, according to Jesuit Joseph Marcoux, the author of an 1853 Iroquois dictionary, renders it "One who places things in order." Jesuit Jean Andre Cuoq, the author of an 1882 vocabulary of the Iroquois language, translates her name of Tekakwitha as "To put all into place."

—Diego Paoletti

Table of Contents

Book One	1
Book Two	91
References	212

BOOK ONE

†

THE LIFE OF THE GOOD CATHERINE TEKAKWITHA, SAID NOW TO BE SAINT CATHERINE TEKAKWITHA

by
Claude Chauchetiere, S.J.

Chapter 1

The honour and respect I owe to the memory of Father Jean de Brebeuf and the other Jesuit Fathers, who began the Iroquois missions, had obliged me to break a silence of five years. It was a silence that I had kept from what passed at the death and after the burial of her, who the life I am writing. The pressing reasons that I had kept this silence were the slight dispositions I saw in the spirit of the French in believing such great marvels. I was perhaps led too much from my own feelings, as I had much difficulty believing the things I saw before my eyes everyday or to have believed some of the French, who doubted there is faith among the Natives.

The principal reason was the certain difficulties that Father Superior of New France in Quebec had in believing the things when he saw written in a small notebook that I prepared during the year 1680. This was to provide an exact account of them and to know what were from God and what were not. The reasons I had for speaking were from a powerful inclination and a very strong inspiration to shine forth, to no longer withhold myself in obscurity and silence.

This truth is worthy of being known all over the land that God was the first to publish from ordinary signs, which He serves to make known to the living of the merit and glory of the dead. I want to say the cures of the afflicted, the revelations, the visions, and the public approbations over the course of the years and all the testimonies we find in the process for the canonization of the saints, which are all found today gathered in Catherine Tekakwitha. One of the reasons was not to deprive the missionaries of the reward that God gave to the labours. This was the extraordinary appearance of virtue and Christianity among the Natives that is so often attacked by slanderous tongues. This is the reason I have attempted to some particular works as the *Annual Narrative of the Mission of the Sault from its Foundation*. This narration is halved into two books and concerns the perseverance of the Natives, who gave their lives to the faith.

I resolved to take the middle course in order to accord these two opposite sentiments that seemed to be the intention of Catherine Tekakwitha, because she revealed to me in a vision to do paintings for the instruction of the Natives and to serve me to exhorting those who she wanted to have attracted to heaven after her. At the same time, I wrote the journals and they had served for my own conduct. I began this work with incredible difficulty and a yearning at times to leave it, but had I abandoned it would have weighed on my conscience, which would not allow me to live in peace and find rest. Thus, I had to obey what Catherine Tekakwitha asked of me.

Diego Paoletti

The first painting I began was painting a copy of *Pains of Hell*, which was sent to me from Father Francis de Belmont. This painting was very well liked among the Natives and the missionaries had asked me a copy of the painting. The copy was generally approved by everyone. This approval gave me the courage to attempt a portrait of Catherine Tekakwitha, which was the one painting I wanted to accomplish because I had been so strongly inspired by my own comfort and that of others.

I began the portrait one year after her death and there was no other person than myself that I could rely on. I had painted other portraits on leaflets that many others had in their possession, but these portraits were too small and not able to be seen from a distance if placed in a large area. If the leaflets were placed in cabins, the portraits immediately became stained with smoke. I resolved to work on this large image of Catherine Tekakwitha. The painting presently resides in the Church of Saint Francis Xavier, serving to provide instruction about the life and morals of Catherine Tekakwitha. The portrait was placed beside the painting of the *Four Ends of Man*, along with the moral paintings of Father Michel Le Nobletz. To facilitate the explanation of this great painting, I created a small book where all the actions of Catherine Tekakwitha are illustrated through painting. These included the healing of the sick and the devotions that were customarily held at her grave. In 1682, we began to instruct through the use of paintings, which greatly pleased the Natives.

These marvels could not last for long without shining forth, first at La Prairie de la Madeleine and then at the Mission of Lachine. It was not my intention to introduce Catherine Tekakwitha to the French. At the time, I was also the Pastor at La Prairie and left in a volume of the *Lives of the*

Saints, a small book of some principal and most edifying actions of those that have marked her life.

Father Bruyas found the book *Lives of the Saints* and opened it to read about the lives of some saints in order to make them known in his sermon to the Natives. On that day, Rene Cuillerier had come to the Sault to hear the mass and did not want to leave without having greeted the Father. This politeness gave the Father the occasion to speak to him concerning the book. They admired the spirit of God, who guided Catherine Tekakwitha during her lifetime and blessed His divine goodness in having made known to them such a great marvel. From this time onward, the name of Catherine Tekakwitha began to be invoked at Lachine, just as it had been for over a year at La Prairie de la Madeleine.

The cures brought about the invocation of the name of Catherine Tekakwitha and the desire of the French to know her virtue was the cause of a longer and clearer recital of what Catherine Tekakwitha had done throughout her life. Almost a year of inquiries and interrogations were conducted among many people in order to verify what had been said about this virtuous girl. The witnesses asked were the person that instructed her, her companion, the sister with whom she had spent a winter in the forest, the missionaries, and especially her spiritual director Father Pierre Cholenec. The French of La Prairie had seen part of what had been written about her. These and several other witnesses rendered believable the actions attributed to her during the two years that she lived at the Sault. Father de Lamberville had baptized her among the Macquas and wrote to the Fathers at the Mission of the Sault regarding Catherine Tekakwitha's manner, both before and after her baptism, during which time he had known her. From his letters we were able to compose her life when she lived among the Macquas.

At last, an incredible occurrence that was without precedent occurred that demanded testimony greater than that of any man. We have one such lasting for fifteen years following Catherine's death, after she had received the sacraments. All the things that she touched during her life have been seen to cure the ailing. These are things such as the crucifix that was placed in her hands when she was buried, her blanket, the earth from her grave, and the plate from which she ate. They have been seen to be able to suddenly restore health. Simply the invocation of her name has relieved people from temptations of the flesh.

In 1681, the Bishop Francis Montmorency de Laval returned to the mission, his last visit having been in 1676, and was told of Catherine Tekakwitha's early miraculous cures. Bishop Jean-Baptiste de Saint-Vallier, the subsequent Bishop, gave his respects at her tomb with three Ecclesiastics recognizing the virtue that she had for aiding those who had invoked her. Religious communities have asked favours of God through her intercession. The French and the Natives have continued to honour her, which provided them with consolation for their souls and relief for their bodies. Several places in France have honoured her for some years now and the missionaries of the Islands of America have invoked her. What is still more amazing is that several people often had the same thought of invoking her without having spoken of it to one another. They discovered that the same spirit had guided them when grace was accorded to them.

A part of her due praise is a result of the exemplary life led by the Sisters of Catherine at the Sault, which they still lead at the mission even today. They began to be recognized after the death of this good servant of God. There are some that have really imitated her, and they died as if predestined, and their lives have since been known. The women still living sanctify themselves by imitating Catherine Tekakwitha so as to live as good Christians. When they die, we see the relationship between their lives and that of Catherine Tekakwitha. Both the men and the women have had their part in this imitation. Several girls have gone to heaven bearing the precious joyousness of virginity because of her.

Finally, the Father Superior from Quebec wrote on Friday the seventeenth of April, 1693, the anniversary day of the death of Catherine, about the virtues of this girl and the cures that followed. After this prediction I had, I am composing a story of her life for myself and for some others who want to know the history of her life in advance and to have her glorified in this world.

Chapter 2

Before Catherine Tekakwitha came to the Mission of Saint Francis Xavier of the Sault, where the Iroquois had already professed the Christian religion for twenty-five or thirty years, Our Lord seemed to have prepared the place for this virtuous girl. He began in 1667, when He inspired Father Pierre Rafeix to go to the already established settlement of La Prairie de la Madeleine and make there a sort of a Parish for the French and a mission for the Natives. Then, Father Rafeix worked to create a resting place for those who came down from the above missions. When peace was made, some of the Natives came from the side of Montreal to hunt, and these hunters supported the foundation of the mission. They would pass the winter there with the French, and three to four cabins were built there for the Natives. The missionaries left the land of La Prairie to settle on a land a league and one quarter higher. They did this because they had planted only corn on the land, which rendered it no longer fertile enough to support their needs. The missionaries settled on this land granted to the Jesuits, which was the Sault Saint Louis or the Sault Saint Francis Xavier from the name of the mission. God had taken seven years to cultivate this new Church, where we saw as many Christians as fervent as those from the primitive Church.

It was at the mission that God wanted to relieve me of a great interior affliction from which I had been suffering for about a year. God gave led me to place my foot in this such a holy mission in 1677, but the great grace that God gave me was through my relationship with Catherine Tekakwitha. Three or four months after my arrival, He had brought Tekakwitha to this place from the land of the Macquas, where she had been born.

The mother of Tekakwitha was a good Christian Algonquin who the Iroquois had taken at Three Rivers during the wars against the Hurons and Algonquins. Fortunately, this poor captured Algonquin was married to an Iroquois; and from this marriage, was born Tekakwitha, which was a marriage between a Christian woman and heathen man. Her mother, whose baptismal name I do not know, also had a son. She lived with her husband and children at Caughnawaga. It was a small village of the Turtle clan of the Macquas, who were one of the five nations of the Iroquois.

Smallpox had ravaged Caughnawaga and caused the death of many children and adults. This tragedy had perhaps obliged the Natives to make peace with the French. The mother of Tekakwitha died and left her two children with only the regret of having left them without them being baptized. It was said that she was a devoted Christian and that she prayed until her death, which perhaps obtained the grace of baptism for her daughter and provided us with the grace of possessing a saint. The other child died, and only Tekakwitha remained. It was thought that she too would die at the age of four years old, because she had also been afflicted with smallpox. This illness bestowed upon her the blessing of virginity. Her face, before unmarked, had become ruined with the scars left from the smallpox. She had almost lost her eyesight, because her eyesight had been severely damaged from her illness and she thus could not endure strong light. This prompted her to remain covered in her blanket and favoured the desire to remain unknown. She often thanked Our Lord for this grace and saying this incommodity was a grace, because if she had been good looking, she may have been more sought after by the young men and done like the other girls, who abandoned themselves to sin.

She had never done anything that might offend God, because from the age of six or seven, she began to possess a certain natural modesty, which is the guardian of chastity. Her good nature and the care her mother took of this little one when she was alive influenced her and made her grow in wisdom. She considered herself a great sinner during her life, because it seemed as if she had a stain on her body and was very careful to hide it.

Chapter 3

The natural inclination for the girls to appear attractive would make them place great value on bodily ornaments. This is the reason that Native girls of seven or eight years old are very attached to shell beads. The mothers spent sometimes a good part of the time combing their hair and braiding into a single plait. This was done to signify that one was not married. They see to it that their ears are well pierced and thus pierce them at birth. Their faces are painted and they cover themselves with shell beads when they are going to dance.

The relatives, who cared for Tekakwitha when her mother died, had decided that she should marry early and encouraged all these small vanities, but she had a natural indifference to such things. Because she was not baptized, the little Tekakwitha was still not a Christian. She was still a small tree without flowers or fruits, but this small wild olive tree was growing well and would one day bring beautiful fruits. She was covered with the darkness of heathenism, but in truth she was destined for heaven, because she was very far removed from corruption.

She was a well-behaved child, patient, chaste and innocent. This is the given testimony concerning her from those who knew her from the time she was a small child. They pronounced these words to do in a few words the beautiful praise for Tekakwitha. When someone asked her how she lived among the Iroquois and during the time they had not seen her; that is to say, from the age of seven or eight years old until the time God guided her to the mission, Tekakwitha replied that she lived the same as before they had left. The person who had demanded her was her instructress from the time she arrived and during the two years at the Sault. She had also known her mother, and knew them when they were together in their country. This good Christian was Anastasia Tegonhatsihongo, who said Tekakwitha had no faults from the time she had known them.

The occupation of Tekakwitha was to bring and place the wood in the fire when her aunt ordered her, and to get water when those in the longhouse needed it. When she had nothing to do, she amused herself with small jewels. She would dress herself as the other girls of her age and only to pass the time. She had placed shell bead necklaces around her neck, shell bead bracelets on her arms, rings on her fingers and ornaments in her ears. She wore large and beautiful shell bead belts that were called shell collars. She had made ribbons and strips as the Natives do from the skin of eels, which they would colour red and render them very clean for their hair ribbons. Twenty years later, she wept so much for these actions, and carried out harsh penance to chastise her body, because then she had loved her body more than she should have.

Tekakwitha lived such a life of innocence, and God was preparing to go find her. When peace was made between the Natives and the French, several Jesuit missionaries, Fathers Jacques Bruyas, Jacques Fremin and Jean Pierron, were sent among them to preach the faith. In July 1667, the Fathers arrived in the villages of the Iroquois at a time of drunkenness and were in no condition to receive the Fathers in their large village Tionnontoguen as anticipated, so they had to stay in the village of Caughnawaga, where Tekakwitha lived. The uncle of Tekakwitha was one of the principal elders of the village and received the Jesuit Fathers in his longhouse. Tekakwitha was in the longhouse and was ordered to render some small services to the Fathers. God arranged all these things, and was seemingly acting for Tekakwitha and allowing her to meet the Fathers, who would later confer the grace of baptism to her.

Chapter 4

Tekakwitha had a natural aversion to pleasures and carried no thought of marriage, and as the smallpox had scarred her face, the young people did not think of her. Her relatives wanted to see her established and thus pressured her to marry, but she did not want this for herself. She then became looked upon as an unpleasant slave, who they thought she would become a burden on the longhouse. For some time, they sent her from longhouse to longhouse.

The people who they knew her as a small child said that she had spirit and was skilful, especially with her fingers, in making such objects as the other Natives do. If I would judge from the objects that I saw her make, I say with ease that she had worked skilfully in porcupine and moose skins. She made belts that the Native women would carry wood and wampum belts made of shell beads, which the elders used in negotiating the affairs of the nation. Another occupation of the

Native women was the sewing that they had learned from both the slaves who were with them or the women from Europe. She was skilful in making ribbons, which the Natives make from eel skins or tree barks. These she coloured red with the glue from sturgeons, which is often employed among the Iroquois. She knew more than the Iroquois girls because she made baskets and buckets used to carry water. In this manner, her skills had always kept her with something to be occupied with. She sometimes made a hollow tree trunk for grinding corn, mats from tree bark and poles to stack the corn. Her everyday occupations were to peel the corn, to make the sagamite and the Native bread, search for water, carry wood and also fill the plates with food and serve them.

Tekakwitha was infirm, but she was always the first to be at work. Before she was baptized, she would pass some years doing the everyday occupations of the Native life. She remained at her longhouse without visiting others and she was not of the malicious talk of others. She was not indolent or proud and was not attached to her dreams, which were common vices experienced by the other girls her age. It was said that from her innocent childhood, she did not want to assist at the dances nor the games and on several occasions she had shown prudence. She was naturally timid nature and appeared only when it was necessary. She never showed any cruel spirit and would not endure to see anyone, even a slave, being harmed. This was because she thought it a sin to see a man tortured.

Chapter 5

The Iroquois say that marriage is not only an agreement between two persons. They would intend to live together, both being congenial, but is a certain agreement from a union of friendship and is strengthen by giving in marriage of a child. This is often done when the child is born. They did this when Tekakwitha was still little, perhaps only about eight years old.

They wanted to give her in marriage to a boy scarcely older than her. They were almost of the same disposition, as the boy also had no thoughts of marriage. It was only in name what the relatives of Tekakwitha had pretended it to be. If God had wanted peace to be made when Tekakwitha was only about eight years old and if she known of the faith, she would have then renounced the flesh and embraced the state for which she was destined. Instead, she was later to pass through other trials, which have made us admire what God had wanted for this good girl.

When she was of the age to be married, her aunts had a young man enter in her longhouse and they told him to sit next to her. They had told Tekakwitha to offer him some sagamite. They had pretended that he spoke of marrying her and they wanted to oblige her to follow him as a husband. Tekakwitha left the longhouse and hid in the fields. This marriage was pressed again and they tempted her, but then this girl hid cleverly behind a cache of corn. Anastasia Tegonhatsihongo, who instructed her at the Sault, told me this. She had known Tekakwitha from the age of four. When her relatives wanted to oblige her to marry, which she resisted with confidence and firmness, they had finally left her to herself. However, it is to believe she was not treated well in the longhouse, where the relatives were frustrated by their hopes of having her married. It was about this time when the Mission of the Macquas was founded and peace was made with the Iroquois.

Tekakwitha had tried to please the relatives of her longhouse in all other matters. She was a good worker and was peaceful and pleasant when she had wanted to make them laugh. They had never complained about her and enjoyed her presence. She was never offended when they said they did not know what to do with her, because she did not want to marry, or when they said that she was not well done. Her good nature had exempted her during this time from committing many sins, for which she would have otherwise fallen if she did not have a natural patience.

Chapter 6

The Fathers Fremin, Bruyas, Pierron and some other Jesuit missionaries had passed some years among the Macquas without having known Tekakwitha. This was partly to the malice of her uncle, who did what he could to prevent his people from going to pray to God at the Sault, even though he allowed them to pray in their own village. Her timid nature was perhaps why she did not attempt to go see the Fathers for instruction.

When Father Jacques de Lamberville was among the Macquas, which God had thrown His merciful eyes on her and the longhouse of Tekakwitha, because this longhouse had received the Fathers when a few years before they brought the faith to the land of the Iroquois. Tekakwitha passed eighteen years in infidelity and then God sent her an illness to have her cured from sin and inspired Father de Lamberville to go instruct this girl toward baptism. It was

CATHERINE TEKAKWITHA: BOOK ONE

spring and they went according to their custom to cultivate their fields. Tekakwitha had gone many times, which was not out of habit of her staying in the longhouse and doing nothing while the others worked, but was due to an injury to her foot that had obliged her unable to walk for a few days. The Father knew that no one in that longhouse was idle. He did not want to enter the longhouse, especially since the uncle of Tekakwitha did not like the French. The Father had before passed Tekakwitha's longhouse, but then felt inspired to enter. He turned back and entered her longhouse, where he found Tekakwitha. This was a most pleasing encounter for the girl, because she wanted to speak to the Father, but she did not have the courage to go to him.

The Father had found a treasure where he did not expect to find one. The first words Tekakwitha said to the Father revealed the sentiments of her heart, but she explained to the Father what her uncle might do to have kept her from being baptized because he feared she would do as all the others had done and leave the country. The Father exhorted her and was content for the time to have her come to the chapel to pray. This first exhortation had a great effect, because God had given such a blessing. When Tekakwitha was well, she did not fail to go there and pray to God.

There were two places in the world that she went, her cabin and the chapel. She had persevered until her death to practice at these two places, and those who sought her went to the chapel or to the cabin to find her. At first, they had caused her no trouble. They had let her pray as the others did and some believed that her longhouse was not opposed to the prayer, because the mother of Tekakwitha was a good Algonquin and prayed until her death, and they had become accustomed to seeing her pray.

After Tekakwitha persevered for some time to pray as a catechumen, Father had thought of baptizing her. He wanted to proceed with the matter, as it was an event of importance to baptize an adult Iroquois. The Father moderated the desire he had of baptizing her, because he saw her as being fervent, devoted and in possession of the qualities of an excellent Christian. He feared to deprive God of a soul so dear to Him if he deferred this baptism too long. He had made inquiries for some days into the life and morals of Tekakwitha. The relatives of Tekakwitha's longhouse and the people of the village had spoken well of her. All the Christians rejoiced that the Father resolved to baptize Tekakwitha. She had experienced extraordinary joy when the news of her impending baptism was brought to her. She had learned her prayers with hastiness and with eagerness, which was truly marvellous. It was the fear of baptism that could have left it deferred, because she thought she perhaps did not have enough instruction. The Father had chosen the day of Easter and the chapel for such a solemn baptism. Tekakwitha was baptized together with two others with all the ceremonies of the Church. She was baptized with the name of Catherine.

Many of the Native girls before and after her were called with that name, but not one has filled it in the manner of the good Catherine Tekakwitha. La Prairie possesses the precious remains of Catherine Ganneaktena, who came from Oneida and was the foundation stone of the mission and the Confraternity of the Holy Family there. Another Catherine had died at the Sault and the age of thirteen, in which she lived a life as innocent as of an angel and died as a victim of her virginity. These two individuals were examples for all the Natives and Christians of the Mission of the Sault alike, but the good Catherine Tekakwitha had shone forth as a sun between the stars. From the time she appeared there, she had raised herself above all Christians of the mission.

The Holy Spirit entered Tekakwitha through her baptism and she became His spouse. He had placed her within the ranks of the elite souls and raised her in four years to the highest sanctity. He had left her two years in her longhouse to overcome the infidelity in her country, because to have served as example to the new Church of the Macquas and increase the merit of Catherine, which led her virtue to be proven in many ways.

Chapter 7

We have seen Natives become indifferent almost as soon as they were baptized, because they did not have the courage to consider human respect. The demon would attempt to persuade the newly baptized to have them lose their grace as soon as they received it.

It is a miracle when a Christian perseveres in the country of the Iroquois. Catherine had practiced her faith in such a manner, which her confessor admits she never once lessened from her original fervour. Everyone saw her extraordinary virtue, from the heathens to the faithful. The Christians saw her exactitude in obeying the rules of life. The Father had told her to go everyday to the prayers of the morning and evening and every Sunday to assist mass. The Father told her what she must avoid. These were the dream feasts, the dances and the other gatherings among the Natives that are contrary to purity. These general rules were good for the others, but Catherine had practiced all of this before her baptism. The Father gave her some particular directions and regulated the prayers that she should say, as well as the practices of virtue to embrace. Catherine had such vigour to live in this manner. The Father admired her, while at the same regretting that he was not able to send her to the Sault. Father de Lamberville had written to a Jesuit Father at the Mission of the Sault after the death of Catherine, saying that he often examined the manner of this new Christian and asking if she did what he asked of her. He affirmed, after well examining her that she did not lessen in her virtuosity from when she became a Christian. It is to believe that this girl acted only from natural goodness, because the first two years of her Christianity she had a much rough novitiate where she showed great virtues.

Chapter 8

There are two sorts of persecutors that are opposed to the intentions of the good Christians, who wanted to serve God as they should, of which some are hidden and others appear. The demon will surpass all these when God permits. From the beginning, Catherine overcame the demon of impurity and sin. The very shadows of them would make her afraid. She was always faithful in evading the occasions of sin and would have no difficulty in avoiding it. We must consider that she had a particular grace from God, which He sent to her to make her His spouse.

Her relatives began to persecute her because she was a Christian and that she had become indolent and did not work in the fields on Sundays. They had expressed disapproval regarding this pretended negligence and later mistreated her in various ways. This is a common manner in this country to make her abandon the Rosary. Catherine said she would rather die than to abandon it. There were some who did not have the courage to declare themselves when they were the only Christians in their longhouses, but Catherine showed an extraordinary firmness of spirit when the children pointed their fingers at her and no longer called her with her Native name, Tekakwitha. They would call her with the name, Christian. This was in derision as one would speak to a dog, and this lasted for such a long time that they forgot her name. They gave her the name Christian, because she was the only one baptized in her longhouse. Tekakwitha was far from having been afflicted with contempt that they had showed towards her, and was content to lose her name.

She had so much to suffer from the derision of the enemies of prayer and her uncle. One day, they wanted her to surrender her good resolutions. A young man with a hatchet was sent into the longhouse by her uncle to pretend to kill this Christian. It was perhaps with the intention of terrifying her, and perhaps to have her refrain from leaving and follow the others that the Great Macqua brought to live at La Prairie.

At last, the last persecution she had suffered was a pure calumny to send her to the despair of her salvation, and to place an end to the spirit that the Father, who he had directed Catherine, had upon her. It was in the spring and during the hunting season when she went with her relatives and uncle. The wife of one of the hunters did not like Catherine, perhaps because her virtuous life was in contrast to the different life that this woman led. This woman examined all the actions and words of Catherine in order to find some faults with them.

It is a manner common among the Natives to treat an uncle as a father and call him the same name as the father.

One day, Catherine was speaking of this old man in the presence of others, and she had referred to him without the name of father or my father. The woman heard this and hastily judged Catherine. This woman went to Father de Lamberville, who he had such esteem for Catherine, saying that she had sinned with her husband.

The Father examined the motivations of the woman and reproached her severely for her slanderous tongue. Then the Father spoke to Catherine. He instructed her on sin and the pains of hell, which God has prepared as punishment. He told Catherine about this woman coming to see him and of her accusation. He asked Catherine about the matter and she replied firmly and modestly that she had never fallen into this sin, neither on this occasion nor any other. She was not afraid of being damned, but she was afraid of not having enough courage to be killed instead of going to work in the fields on Sundays. She believed that she had not done enough by going entire days without eating, because the others had hidden all there was to eat in the longhouse and left her with nothing that was prepared for the day. They thought the hunger might convince her to go in the fields to work.

Chapter 9

We had already seen the rare example of faithfulness in a good Christian woman who was at the Mission of Loreto. This woman, Mary Tsiaouentes, had gone to visit the Macquas and some drunken people closed her in a cabin and attempted to have her drink with them. As a virtuous Christian, she did not want to drink, but they threw her on the ground and poured liquor into her mouth. She resisted and spat it out in their faces and thus gained the victory.

When Catherine struggled with others, she would always conquer them with prayer. When some extraordinary incident arrived, Catherine sought the Father to say all of her troubles. She demonstrated the ingenuousness of her spirit and the simplicity of her relationship with God. This was her spirit of obedience and her profound humility.

The Father studied her soul, so that nothing might be missing in her conduct. He had always proposed two things to her. This was to leave the country, where she was not able to gain her salvation in peace, and the other was to have a continual desire for prayer. The first proposal had frightened her, because she knew her uncle would never consent to her departure, but the other proposal pleased her greatly, because in this world, Our Lord Jesus was her only means of consolation.

Father de Lamberville made her practice the instruction that he gave her, because when he instructed her he led her to the chapel and made her offer all her crosses to Our Lord. We could not say enough about the great progress that Catherine made under such this direction. The Holy Spirit led her in everything and in such manner that she had pleased both God and the world, because even the worst admired her and the best found in her a worthy model. However, this life had presented her with some falls and rendered her perseverance very difficult. Catherine would have wanted to leave her country, but did not have the courage to talk when she saw the Christians and the Great Macqua, who came from La Prairie to the Iroquois. She was consoled when they came, but when they left without her, she was extremely afflicted. It was not until the following year that she had obtained the desired opportunity to fulfill her plan. Her uncle had adopted another girl, who lived with Catherine and her aunts, but she would later go to live with her husband in the Mission of the Sault. The zeal of these recent converts, to have attracted their relatives and friends to the Sault, would inspire her sister with the same thoughts as regard to Catherine. She then made her plan known to her husband, of which he gave his consent.

Chapter 10

I have considered Catherine, until now, as a lily among thorns, but now we will see how God transplanted this beautiful lily and placed it in a garden filled with other beautiful flowers. It is to say, in the Mission of the Sault where there have been and will always be full of beautiful flowers, which are virtuous people renowned for their virtue. There were even roses; that is to say, martyrs from the Mission of the Sault, who were burned in Onondaga because they would not leave the prayer or to live as the Huguenots in the village that the Ministers founded near Fort Orange. This was in imitation of the Catholics, who built the Mission of Saint Francis Xavier for the instruction of the Natives in the Christian faith, the true religion. The fervour was very strong at the Sault when God wanted to guide Catherine there, and He inspired the Christian Natives there to make apostolic visits to their country, where they brought Christianity to their relatives.

One of the most successful of these Christian Natives was Ogeratarihen or Louis Garonhiague, who had such a great relation with Catherine. His name, Garonhiague, meant Hot Powder or Hot Ashes. He was married, but he had never received the sacrament, because he was not then a Christian. He lived peacefully with his wife, who had an excellent disposition and they lived together from the age of eight without ever having been separated. His temper was violent and fiery, but his wife calmed him with her gentleness.

His fiery-nature was why he left Oneida. He had a dispute that raised his temper with someone at the time of a migration of the village. This was the death of his brother. In his anger, he was persuaded that it was the French and went to Montreal to avenge the death of his brother. However, he learnt along the way that the cause of death was from another side. He then adopted the resolution to remain at the Mission of the Sault, where he spent some time and pleased everyone with his good conduct. His wife, Mary Garhi, joined him and she was even more inclined to Christianity than her husband. He had asked to be instructed and be baptized with all his family. This baptism of the Chief of the Oneidas was a great act of God for the mission, because many Oneidas would come to visit Hot Ashes and would then become Christians. They came more and more, and it became apparent to choose Hot Ashes as the fourth Chief of the Sault. Until the death of Hot Ashes, his eloquent speech, his authority and his admirable restraint always exemplified his conduct.

His ability in speaking and his powers of persuasion were a great aid to the instruction of others to a good life. He had employed paintings from his book called the *Book of the Ignorants*. He had attracted many people to Christianity and converted them in his cabin from this sort of exhortation. He was given, for his great success, the paintings representing the actions of the most excellent Christians, who lived at the mission under the example of the life and actions of Catherine Tekakwitha. Many others imitated him in aiding the missionaries to instruct those who had recently arrived.

He was extremely charitable, especially to widows, and constantly encouraged others in the village to care for them. When there was work to be done in the fields of the poor, he was always the first to lead by example, and the service he had rendered in the village was well known when they lost such a great Chief. When rumours of war began to spread throughout New France, Hot Ashes did not hesitate to side himself with the French. Before having left, he decided to go to Catherine's grave for some earth to carry with him. This was to give him the grace to come back in good health, as she had done in saving his wife, who was dying at childbirth and recovered when the blanket of Catherine was placed over her.

He would carry his catechisms and paintings to the forest, because to instruct everyone that he came in contact or he could attract. When he had made converts, he would become their godfather at baptism, because to have the right to rebuke those if they would do wrong. Father Pierre Millet was then at Fort Catarakoui and wrote to Father Bruyas, who was then the Superior of the Mission of the Sault, to send the Christians of the Sault when hunting, because of the fruit they have done from their words and examples.

When it became necessary to engage in battle against the Senecas, Hot Ashes told his wife to always remain a good

Christian, because she asked of him for the preceding two years to live in marriage as brother and sister. He said little in leaving, but his heart said so much through his commending himself to prayers. He left her with their young child, who was infirm in body yet strong in spirit. Only two people from our village died in this battle; Hot Ashes was one of them. Hot Ashes died while praying to God on Monday July 14, 1687. This was the man who God had chosen to take Catherine from the Iroquois, so she would serve God in peace at the Mission of the Sault.

Hot Ashes went to the Macquas with the brother-in-law of Catherine and a Native from the Huron Mission of Loreto, with the intention of bringing back someone that God had predestined. On their arrival, they went to the Chapel of Saint Peter in Caughnawaga and as was the custom, began their visit with prayer.

Father de Lamberville received these three visitors in his cabin. He had so much love for such visits and considered these Christians from the Sault as being similar to angels from heaven. We saw the spirit of Christianity and the mortification of their passions were depicted on the faces of these new apostles. This attracted more people than what we saw. The elders were the first to meet these visitors from the Sault, and the uncle of Catherine was at Fort Orange. It was a circumstance that God had facilitated in favour of Catherine, allowing her to leave more with ease.

Hot Ashes began to speak when the audience was of sufficient size. He said to them that before he was a warrior and an Oneida Chief, and he had acted like them. He was nothing but a dog in those days and began only to act like a man in the last few months. He also said many other touching things, of which Catherine profited more than anyone else.

The elders left one after another until the preacher was almost alone. Catherine could not separate from these visitors. She had testified to the Father that she must go with them even though may cost her life.

Father de Lamberville had spoken to Hot Ashes and his companions. The Chief replied that there was a place for her in the canoe, because he intended to go to Oneida and preach the faith among the Iroquois nations. The resolution was decided upon and placed into action and Catherine secretly embarked with the two companions of Hot Ashes. They left the day after Hot Ashes and his companions arrived there.

Chapter 11

God had guided the saints along roads unknown to men and guided Catherine to the Sault in an extraordinary manner without having been discovered. When it had become known that the three visitors from the Sault were gone, and that Catherine was not in the longhouse, suspicion was raised. They hastened to carry the news to Catherine's uncle, even though he was an evil man and an enemy of those who came from the Sault. Her uncle quickly left to find the travelers while returning to the village.

He searched thoroughly for his niece, but the three travelers eluded the old man through disembarking from the river and hiding in the forest. When they were near Fort Orange, her brother-in-law decided to go to get bread. He left Catherine with this good Native from the Mission of Loreto, who had lived many years in continence with his wife. As her brother-in-law left, her uncle approached. Her brother-in-law had seen the old man but he was too close to avoid him without being suspicious. Because Catherine's uncle did not recognize his son-in-law, they then both continued on their separate way. When her brother-in-law returned, he told her of his adventure. Catherine had seen it always as a particular sign to her from the providence of God. She was encouraged to abandon herself entirely to God and profit from the occasions He gave salvation to her.

Her voyage was a continual prayer and the joy she felt when she was approaching the Mission of the Sault could not be explained. This is a young Native girl of twenty-one years old, who has remained saintly and pure, and triumphed over vice and infidelity. Here is the Saint Genevieve of New France, the treasure of the Sault and whom has sanctified the roads from the Sault to the Macquas, where many predestined souls have passed after her. When she found herself far from her own country and there was no longer to fear her uncle, she gave herself entirely to God. She promised in the future to do all that was to be most agreeable to Him. She had arrived in the autumn of 1677 after having made an uninterrupted voyage because of her great desire to arrive at her destination.

Father de Lamberville gave letters to Catherine to bring with her, which he wrote to Fathers Fremin and Cholenec at the mission. When she arrived, she placed the letters in their hands. After reading them, they were delighted to receive a treasure, because the words in the letter were, "I am sending you a treasure, guard it well!"

Her face had said more than the letters. We could not say the joy she had then in the land of light and freed from spiritual troubles. She was content of having good companions and to hear everyday several masses, and especially having to receive often Communion. She was delivered from the persecutions endured in her own country and in her longhouse, because she was not able to serve God as she had wanted. She arrived at the Sault when the chapel was a cabin made only of bark, where she satisfied her devotion and who was more devoted than the older Christians.

Chapter 12

A short time before the arrival of Catherine, when we had wanted to say a person was a good Christian, we would say that the person resembled Catherine Ganneaktena, who is buried at La Prairie. The defeat of the nation of the Cats was a blessing for Ganneaktena, the Erie woman of whom we speak, because on becoming an Iroquois that she became a Christian. She was taken as a slave and given to the Oneidas and her life was without reproach. She was never stained with the vices common among the infidels. She was married to a good Huron warrior and his name was Francis Tonsahoten. He kept the promise he had made at baptism until his death; that is, of refraining from drunkenness.

In 1667, Ganneaktena spent the winter in Montreal. She often went to the chapel and assisted with the ceremonies at Christmas. Father Rafeix, who began to build a chapel in La

Prairie, had invited and took the care to instruct them. The following spring, he brought them to Quebec, where Father Chaumonot had instructed, and baptized them. After she was baptized, she did not seem to want to remain among the French, because her husband was determined to return to their country. She succeeded and obliged her husband to go to La Prairie. They had lived with Father Rafeix until the beginning of the summer when her husband built their cabin. The place was an advantage for fishing and hunting and they also cleared the land to sow corn. This was the beginning of the mission that would be the Sault.

Her generosity made her loved by everyone, and her cabin was the refuge for anyone who was afflicted. They were the two first Christians of the mission. They had lived in a religious manner and every form of devotion was practiced. She was the first that God chose to establish the Holy Family among the Iroquois, for this reason Father Pierron had given her a Rosary of the Holy Family.

While working in the fields in the hot sun, she was seized with a headache, but it caused her joy through the hope that she would soon see her desires fulfilled. She was in continual devotion by saying the Rosary with those who came to see her during her illness. During the first days of her illness, she had wanted ardently to go to heaven and asked of God only to die in peace with all the sacraments. She had died on Monday, November 6, 1673. Everyone was struck with grief when she died. They had called her the Mother of the Poor, the Good Christian and the Pillar of the Faith.

A year before, the winter of 1688, Francis Tonsanhoten died as a good Christian at the Sault. When the village was changed, he went to the Sault and he gave his land to the building of a bark cabin for the chapel as a testimony of the affection he had for the faith. He was called the Father of the Faithful, because he was the first Christian Native who had lived at La Prairie and the Sault.

After God had taken her, He brought Catherine Tekakwitha, who had virtue that was to render her incomparable. The name of Catherine was with great veneration among the Natives, but this name became even more admired when this young virgin was sanctified at the Sault.

Chapter 13

The life that the good Catherine Tekakwitha had led for the next two years was to serve as an example for the most fervent Christians of Europe. The spirit of Saint Catherine of Sienna and the other saints with this name was revived in her from a particular guidance from God. God had made known to her at times the secrets of a spiritual life. She had the spirit of penance to an eminent degree and found joy in being united with God before knowing the other two stages.

Catherine Tekakwitha arrived at the Sault in the autumn of 1677. She lived with her adopted sister and her brother-in-law, who took care of her until she died. A part of their support for her was easy for them, because she was a good worker and did enough on her part to live. Clothing was most difficult to find and would oblige several of the Native girls to marry against their desire to imitate the Sisters from

France, which was to practice the Evangelical Counsel. This practice is more a heroic virtue for the Natives than the French. Several Native girls tried to imitate Catherine, but only a few persevered unless they were widows, even though young, that they generously renounced a second marriage.

When Catherine came, in the cabin there was a venerable Christian woman whom God had gave her a rare talent of instructing. She was called Anastasia Tegonhatsihongo, and knew Catherine from the land of the Macquas and had seen there Catherine's mother. This old acquaintance, the desire of Catherine to know what was most agreeable to God, and the talent Anastasia had for instruction had attached Catherine to her.

Catherine first learned the ordinary exercises of the mission for the feast and working days. She learned more in one week than the others had in several years. She would always have the Rosary with her, whether in the cabin, in the fields or in the forest. We would see her with the Rosary in her hand and with her dear instructress, when she came and went while carrying her charge of the wood. The lowest occupations were raised from the fervour and spirit with which Catherine did them. She had never separated from Anastasia, because she learned more when the two were alone together cutting wood than at any other place. Catherine's actions made Anastasia say that Catherine never lost sight of God.

The content of their conversations was the life and morals of good Christians. When Catherine heard that Christians do certain things, she sought to practice them like a bee gathers pollen from all sorts of different flowers. The fear she had of offending God would make her love solitude. She did not frequently associate with people of her own gender, because she did not want any other acquaintances than those that could lead her to perfection. In this, her prudence often appeared admirable. Catherine separated from a girl with she was attached because she saw that this girl was arrogant, but Catherine made this separation without having made it known to her.

The manner Anastasia did to instruct Catherine was to ask of her what she had done in her country during the time that they were separated. She had asked Catherine if she did not want to marry, because she was already passed the marriageable age. Catherine told her of her thoughts concerning these things. She had always done as among the Iroquois, always knowing to give the idea of what she was and confessing her ignorance. When Anastasia had spoken to her of slander and stated that it must be avoided, Catherine asked her what it was. We must not be astonished that she did not know slander, either in speculation or in practice, because we had never heard Catherine speak badly of any person; not even those who had unjustly accused her.

Chapter 14

Her grief was who would teach her of what is most agreeable to God in such a way that she could do it. She would sometimes be grieved, because of Father Cholenec. She had said that he would hide something from her, which he made the others practice and he would not come to see her to instruct in the things she must do for pleasing God.

She talked of her instructress, who insisted too much on her getting married. If we told that her marriage was necessary for salvation, she would of have embraced it, but she doubted it very much and believed that there was something more perfect and more heroic, because she had reflected on the lives that the missionaries had led among them or upon the lives that the Sisters had led among the French. In this spirit of perfection and transforming men into angels, she considered her body as miserable as mud and again as her enemy.

She considered the differences between the life she led among the Iroquois and the life she saw us leading at the Sault. Her fear of falling into the disorders of her country increased. This gave her more passion to continue in the practices, which she had come to learn from. An accident was to confirm all of her thoughts. One day, she was cutting down a tree to get wood for the fire and in falling, the tree hit her so violently that one of its branches threw her to the ground and stunned her. They believed she was dead. When she had regained her senses, she had said, "My Jesus, I thank you of having saved me from this accident." She arose immediately after having said those words and took her hatchet and wanted to continue working, but they did not let her and made her rest.

She said that God had again pressed her life to do penance and that she must employ her time well. Another circumstance was strongly favoured to the intention of Catherine. In the village there was a good Christian and a very fervent woman named Mary Theresa Tegaiaguenta who had been baptized there. Before she was baptized, she had been married, but was not done in the Rite of the Church. After coming to La Prairie, she would have an incident that would be the cause of her conversion. When she came to the Sault, she would change her life entirely. God gave her to Catherine as a companion. Mary Theresa had the same thoughts as Catherine; that is, to live in the service of God without having to marry.

Simple curiosity was the cause of their first encounter. The first chapel at the Sault was being built and the carpenters were working on the paneling. Catherine and Mary

CATHERINE TEKAKWITHA: BOOK ONE

Theresa walked outside and inside the chapel without speaking and without being known to each other, because Catherine had arrived from the Macquas only in the autumn and this chapel was finished in the spring of 1678. Mary Theresa came from Oneida, where she had not heard of Catherine, but the spirit of the faith had animated and united them perfectly.

They saluted and spoken to each other, and their words were from the sentiments of their hearts. Catherine had asked where the women would be placed in the chapel and Mary Theresa showed the place where she thought they would be. Catherine said that it is true this wooden chapel was not what God asked the most, but that He asked to be within us. She did not merit being in the chapel with the others because she had very often chased Our Lord from her heart, and merited being outside of the chapel with the dogs. This long discourse was mingled with devotional tears. Their hearts had opened gradually while talking and they began to talk of their past lives. So as to talk more leisurely, they sat down at the bottom of the cross, which was placed next to the chapel and on the bank of the river. They told each other all the secrets in their minds. They promised never to be separated from each other and they would together do penance for their sins.

At first, this spirit of penance was inspired in Catherine by her instructress, because of the bad life they lived in their country. Anastasia had spoken often of hell, the great penance done by the first Christians, the voluntarily penance embraced by the Christians and of the necessity they had for penitence. Catherine took these instructions as if she had a great need for them. Although it is certain from all that we have seen of her life that her soul was very innocent. This is why she had taken all of what was instructed to those who are still in the purgative life and as if she were in a union with God, even though she sought only what was most pleasing to God.

Chapter 15

The missionary Fathers, who had guided her in the beginnings of her spiritual life, would leave it to the Holy Spirit several things of which several people were capable of doing, and especially to Catherine. Mary Theresa Tegaiaguenta decided it would be better if there were three of them together, or if they had some other Christian girl with them from whom they could learn all they wanted to know. Mary Theresa said that she knew of one who had lived for a long time at the Mission of Our Lady of Loreto in Quebec, which was from this plan that the Mission of the Sault was formed. Mary Skarichions is the name of this third person we speak of.

Catherine agreed with what her companion wanted and later the three of them assembled at the foot of the cross. Mary Skarichions had spoken first of her desire to be like them. She proposed to adopt the rule of life she saw from the

Sisters while ill in Quebec. She said this would mean that they should never separate, they would dress the same, and if possible, live in the same cabin.

They chose Heron Island as their dwelling place. All this was made as part of their deliberation, because they had little concept of what constituted a religious life in a convent. Catherine thanked the one who spoke with tears of joy in her eyes. She begged her to hide nothing from her, which would be most pleasing to God. The other two always had the resolution to give themselves entirely to God and never to marry, but none of them profited as much as Catherine. She always followed the rules of life taught to her by her confessor.

Her practice was to go to the chapel at four o'clock in the morning. In the winter, she would walk barefoot through the snow to go to the chapel. Each day, she attended the two masses and frequently visited the Blessed Sacrament. She went to Confession every Saturday. She received Communion as often as possible and she had done her spiritual communion extremely often during the day. Her great devotion and spiritual fervour had placed her in the Holy Family nearly immediately after she arrived from the Iroquois. She was exempted from passing through the trials, which the others who had recently arrived and the newly baptized went through before receiving Communion or being admitted into the Holy Family.

CHAPTER 16

One of the principal signs that what was happening in Catherine that came from God was obedience when these three girls took to the resolution to live as Sisters. When they had arrived at their decision, they went at once to Father Fremin and told him that they had formed an assembly, but they wanted to do nothing without first advising him. He had told them they were too young in the faith for such peculiarity and that Heron Island was too far removed from the village, which all the young people passing to or from Montreal would always be at their cabin. They deemed what the Father said as reasonable and abandoned the idea of their convent on Heron Island.

All this surprised the Father and he thought it was the time to speak to Catherine of the things he could not say to the others. She had come to him in particular, and opening her heart, asking him if it would be absolutely necessary for her to marry to be a good Christian as she had been told by her instructress. The Father had explained the different conditions of life and said to Catherine that God has left us the liberty to decide for ourselves whether or not to marry. This filled her with joy and she decided to no longer inquire about the condition of the life that God had planned for her.

In the beginning of autumn 1678, smallpox covered our village. After it subsided, we were astonished by the few burials.

Catherine entered a renewed fervour when she was preparing for the coming feasts for Christmas and Saint Francis Xavier, who was the patron of the Sault. This was the second Christmas she spent at the Sault, because it was a year and a half since she had come from her country. Father Fremin had given her some rules of life that were much different from the others. He had especially instructed her to retire in the summer when the canoes from Outaouacs would come; that is, she was to stay in her cabin and refrain from going to the side of the river like the others to see their arrival. Also, she was to obey him by never again going to Montreal. It was needed to say something once to her for her to immediately place into practice.

It had become a common adage in the village to say that Catherine was either in her cabin or in the chapel. She prescribed for herself some rules of conduct and being a young Native girl of twenty-two or twenty-three years of age, she should naturally like to be good and be as properly dressed as the others. This consisted of having the hair well-greased, straight and parted or braided in a long plait hung down the back and necklaces of shell beads, moccasins, and beautiful blankets and vests. In a few words, vanity had possessed them. Although Catherine thought she could leave all these things without seeming particular, we had seen from her only thought, as she was not searching for a husband. She had renounced all red clothing and ornaments that the Native girls placed on them. Catherine would wear only a new and simple blue blanket for the days when she would receive Communion. She had accompanied this sacrament very perfectly, which only God had known, but she could not well hide it to her companion, who knew of it in the moments of their greatest fervour together.

The feasts of Saint Francis Xavier and Christmas passed and Catherine was taken to the hunt, where she did as many extraordinary things in solitude as she had done in the village. Her companion, Mary Theresa Tegaiaguenta, was conversing with Catherine concerning the indignation she felt against herself and her sins. One day, Mary Theresa was in the forest and being filled with sorrow at the thought of her sins, which led her to take a handful of cut branches and hit herself on the hands. Another time, she had climbed a tree to obtain some birch bark for some object she was making and she was taken with fear of looking down and seeing many stones because she thought that if she fell, she would and on her head. Then a good thought came to her of confirming all the good resolutions she had taken to serve God, because she had reflected on her fear and blamed herself for having feared death and not the fall to hell. When she came down from the tree, she had tears in her eyes. After she had descended, she sat at the foot of the tree and threw the bark to one side. She gave herself to the good sentiments, which then had possessed her. Catherine took well to what her companion told her. She would take the resolution to do an exercise of devotion everyday, which she could keep during the winter hunt.

Chapter 17

Catherine did all the things without vanity and in the spirit of God. She had continued the same exercises of devotion in the forest as she practiced in the village. She substituted for those she could not do for the exercises of devotion with the ones of her own invention; that is to say, the ones suggested to her by the Holy Spirit.

It seemed as though God was content in having the Natives see that this sort of life could have been sanctified through Catherine. Catherine had only passed one winter on the hunt from when she arrived at the Sault, but she had so well hidden her devotional practices that we reflected upon them only after her death.

This reservation gave rise to occasions of defamation. This winter, she had passed her life as if she were a Sister. In the morning, she had prayed to God with all the others and being a praiseworthy custom of those who went to the hunt.

CATHERINE TEKAKWITHA: BOOK ONE

After the prayers were said, the men ate and went hunting for moose or beaver and did not return to the cabin until the evening. At the cabin, while the hunters were eating, Catherine would hide to say a prayer within herself or vocally, or a combination of the two. Near a stream where those from the cabin would come to get water, she had built a shrine consisting of a cross that she made in a tree. There, she assisted at the mass, because she was not able to hear and joined her intention with those, who were at the village. As she had told her companion, she prayed to her Guardian Angel to be present for her at the mass and bring her fruit. She would return at about nine o'clock in the morning to the cabin, where the women were and when she thought the hunters had left.

She did what she was told, whether to cut wood or make sagamite or to do the ordinary work of the Native women such as making belts from moose skins to carry wood. This she did very skilfully, because it was said that there was nothing the Native women could do that she could not do as well. While at work and during the occupations of the day, she would ask who could sing. She would have them sing some hymns from the chapel or tell of the life of some saint, which they heard in the sermons on Sundays in the village. She would begin by giving them a theme.

Those that were with Catherine regarded her as a saintly girl when she was seen praying with such an angelic modesty. Two or three years after her death of Catherine, her sister said she had respect mingled with joy. This was seen in the chapel before it fell at the Sault, as some wood logs she had cut after she had fell a tree and with two wooden cases, containing wood logs, made by her. Some of them who spoke badly of her about her retirement or of her particular devotions stated that when they would think of Catherine they were struck with tears of devotion and begged her forgiveness.

While the others in the forest had thought only of beavers and martens, Catherine thought only of serving God and imitating Our Lord in poverty, even though poverty had never made her fear of not having a husband. She was poor. She had no vest to wear when she received the Holy Viaticum, but her companion would lend her vest to Catherine to wear. This was the very principal reason why some who had wanted to imitate Catherine did not persevere. They were not enough like her, which we could have admired a faithfulness and a way to act everyday equally, because her life was more than the comprehension of the Native's nature.

Chapter 18

We are now in a great area, of which we have not presently seen the end. Her austerities were divided into those that she had done in the forest and the village. I begin with those she done during the hunt or where they spent the winter. One day, her sister saw that Catherine had gone to get the meat of an animal that someone killed some leagues from the cabin. When they had passed the side of a pond covered with ice, Catherine let her companions pass and she walked for a long time barefoot on the sharp ice of the pond. They saw her falling behind and waited for her, because they thought that she felt unease. Her sister then saw she was barefoot. Catherine, seeing that she had been noticed, put her moccasins on and tried to dissuade them from thinking that she had done something to mortify herself.

They told me also that Catherine could not hide from her companion, that when Catherine went to pray to God as her custom near a small stream, where she had made her place of prayer during the winter hunt. She harshly chastised herself with willow shoots. At the time, they had only willow shoots, and in this country they are very long. This is all the more believed because she already begun to harshly chastise her body in the village. She was not able to do it for long, because she could not endure such cold without a fire. She did this especially on the feast days, during the hunt and completed there with the devotions that she was accustomed to doing at the village.

When she would not go on the hunt in the winter, she would take advantage of her opportunity. They said that on the feast of the Purification, she had walked barefoot in a procession in snow above her knees through her field while she prayed her Rosary several times.

Her companion stated that once, while Catherine was carrying a large load of wood, while wearing a belt of iron with spikes, she slipped on ice and fell down a hill while coming from her field to the village. This fall had pushed the spikes of her belt well into her flesh. She laughed and would not leave her burden, as her companion begged her to do. She went to her cabin and hid her injury so well that no one suspected it.

This spirit of penance was inspired from her first instructress, who she had called her mother. While instructing her one day, she said the fires of hell had caused her more fear than everything what God employed to chastise sin. Catherine was touched and penetrated with the pain for her sins. She did not sleep that night, but when everyone was asleep after the evening prayers, she burned herself from her tips of her toes to her knees with a burning piece of wood. Although her legs were burned, she had spent the rest of the night in the chapel.

Another time, Mary Theresa told Catherine that she wanted to burn herself as a slave and would place a coal of fire between her second toe and the big toe while saying the Hail Mary. Catherine said she also wanted to do as so, but her companion said to Catherine that she would not have the heart to do it, because the pain pierced her when she saw the coal of fire burning the flesh. The next day, she saw Catherine in her cabin and admired her faithfulness, because she had a large hole in her foot and could not have done what she did without feeling great pain.

When we noticed that Catherine would eat nothing on certain days of the week, as on Wednesdays and Saturdays, or when she went to cut wood during the day, we began taking guard of her and would not let her go before the sagamite was ready. Catherine would be evasive sometimes by telling the woman who was at the fire that to stay in the cabin because she had a child to watch. Catherine then had nothing to detain her and would go into the forest. When she was so well guarded and could not leave without being seen, she mortified herself by eating her sagamite mingled with ashes, especially during Lent, the Fridays after Easter and sometimes after she had so much worked during the whole day.

The horror the new Christians of the Sault had for the life they led before their baptism brought them against sin. They did not spare themselves in the practice of great penance. However, Catherine had known nothing of these penances, but no one would tell her, because the weakness of her body had given them pain for her sufferings. Her innocence was great and her fervour was solid. She sought everywhere for herself what the others would not teach her and because of this, while she was in the cabin of her companion to speak of spiritual matters, they talked a long time upon different devotional matters. This they had done one Saturday evening before the bell of the chapel was rung, which was rung every Saturday evening at the mission as an indication to say prayers. In those days, they were accustomed to preparing themselves for Confession on Saturdays and Catherine joined in the customary preparation that I am about to mention.

We knew that Catherine's companion punished herself for her sins with willow shoots, and suggested this as means of atonement to Catherine. Catherine would leave the cabin and go into the cemetery, which was near and would gather a handful of shoots. Then having returned to the cabin, she hid them cleverly under her mat that she sat on. When the first hit of the bell was rung, Catherine and her companion entreated everyone in the cabin to go at the chapel. When the two were alone, they had closed the door from the inside and satisfied their devotion. Catherine was the first on her knees and demanded her companion the grace of not sparing her. Although her companion had wanted to be the first, because fearing they would not have enough time, Catherine persuaded her companion to do as she had begged. After this, they had said a prayer as to their intention and when their zeal was satisfied, they went to the Sault filled with joy, even though their shoulders were covered with blood. They had never found the prayers short as that day and never were they more content. They did not rest until they had found a more appropriate place to continue their harsh devotion. They had chosen a cabin belonging to a Frenchman that sometimes traded with the Natives, but he was living at La Prairie de la Madeleine. This man had left this cabin opened and this place seemed appropriate to them, especially as it was in the middle of the cemetery where a large cross stood beside it.

They chose Saturday as the day to have prepared for their Confession. The method they kept was to make an act of contrition, which the one in prayers taught the Natives, or some other act according to their devotions. Their devotions were to begin with reciting of the Act of Faith as we had done everyday in the chapel. Catherine, who always wanted to be the first in penance, knelt down and received the stripes with willow shoots.

Catherine would always say it was not painful enough and encouraged her companion to hit her harder, although though I knew that the third hit would cause blood to flow. When they came to a pause, they said the Rosary of the Holy Family and divided it with many pauses, which each pause they gave themselves five more stripes and at the end of their devotions they ceased to count the stripes. Then she had disclosed the sentiments from her heart with these words, "My Jesus, I must suffer with you. I love you, but I have offended you. It is to satisfy your justice I am here. Discharge, my God, on me your anger." Sometimes she was not able to speak further, but with her eyes bathed in tears and she finally would often say, "I am extremely touched from the three nails that attached Our Lord to the cross. They are a symbol of my sins." This they would do again every Sunday, with prayers and penance in this cabin in the middle of the cemetery.

When Catherine was touched of the sort, she touched her companion. Her companion would make to Catherine the same supplications, which Catherine had made to her. We had often admired what this faithful companion of Catherine had affirmed, when this saintly girl was in her fervours, she told all her sins to her companion.

She never had anything more grievous on her conscience than when she lived before her baptism. This consisted of not resisted those who brought her to the fields to work on feast days and on Sundays, because she had not suffered martyrdom and often feared death more than sin.

The later part of the year 1679, passed in this manner and Father Fremin was in France for the affairs of the mission. Father Cholenec had the charge of the mission and would have the time only for the general affairs. However, Father Cholenec was certain that they would do nothing, especially concerning the manner of life they wanted to lead without consulting their confessor. As an example, each day Catherine and Mary Theresa would perform some act of devotion, which was proper and conveniently to their plan. The Fathers were surprised at the progress that the new Christians made in all the Christian virtues, but they still did not know everything what passed between Catherine and her companion.

Catherine had fallen ill and was in danger of death, and it was then her companion began to have scruples about letting Catherine die without having told someone of their mortification. She went to Father Cholenec with Catherine's permission, which Catherine voluntarily consented to it. The Father was greatly surprised, but without testifying his astonishment he blamed them for being not prudent. He told them that this imprudence was forgiven in the new Christians and we then instructed and regulated their devotions. Catherine recovered as if the sickness had been more a cause of neglect than a weakness or loss of strength. She continually importuned her confessor and begged him to have pity on her, and permit her to carry out some penances so her body would not win over sins. He permitted her to do some small penances, because the life of the Natives was already full of hardships.

What is admirable is that a girl of twenty-three, who was always ill, was able to accomplish in the four years she lived after her baptism and had done the many things with such a great fervour and pulled strength from her weakness. She did as much as she could with the little we had permitted her. She had demanded permission in her last days of her illness to fast, because it was Holy Week. She did not consider herself to be so weak and three days later she died, but she had in her spirit only her salvation that she thought of night and day. If Catherine would not able to obtain what she asked for, she would place herself in a cramped position so that she could make her body suffer. Anastasia approached her about this behaviour and said to her that she would kill herself doing this sort of thing. Catherine replied laughing, and said that Our Lord suffered much more on the cross and that she had suffered nothing in comparison to Him.

When Catherine recovered from her illness, so to speak, for she had been infirm all her life and was often more sick than well, she again began to do the ordinary work of the Natives and fulfilled herself with penance. She had the thought to hasten her purgatory, because she believed that she had little time to live.

One day, at the beginning of Lent at the Passion of Our Lord while resting herself near a thorn shrub, she was filled with sorrow because she had done nothing for Him. The fervour would lead her to place some branches with thorns among her wood. On arriving at her cabin, she took a handful of these thorns and placed them under the bark that served as her mat. When she went to sleep in the evening, she took out these thorns and spread them on her mat. Then she placed herself on them. The first and second nights passed without any effect, but the third night her body succumbed. The Father saw her and was in doubt of something. She confessed to him and threw the thorns into the fire. They had said that this caused her death. Others say it was when her companion was sent with several other Native girls over the ice along the Great River to La Prairie to bring something, Catherine accompanied her and that she caught a fever, and from this time on that she was never well. We had believed she had died from pneumonia

Chapter 19

The ardent desire of Catherine was to be at the Mission of the Sault, because she could have received Communion. The Natives of the Sault, who had visited the Macquas, were an envy to Catherine when she saw them receive Communion. It was this desire to be united with Our Lord, which had brought her so often to the chapel and made her find the life in the forest an annoyance.

The only consolation in her very great infirmities was to be able to go at the chapel, where she had remained there with the modesty of an angel during whole hours. When she entered the chapel, she would take the Holy Water and reminded herself of her baptism, and she had renewed the resolution taken to live as a good Christian. After having knelt in some corner near the railing and from the fear of distractions from those entering or leaving, which she would cover her face with her blanket and made an act of faith that touched the Real Presence in the Blessed Sacrament.

She also made many interior acts of contrition, resignation and humility, which were according to the inspiration that touched her interiorly. She had asked God for light and strength to well practice virtue. She had prayed for the infidels, and especially her Iroquois relatives, and ended her devotions with the chaplet. She had confidence in this exercise of devotion to her companion, who reported it. If Catherine had not hidden several other beautiful practices that the Holy Spirit taught her, we could more admire the progress that the faith had made in her and in such a short time.

She had a particular time for these visits that brought her to Our Lord five times a day, without ever missing one. The Rosary was recited from two choirs in an exercise during the holy days of which Catherine never neglected this exercise. We could say the chapel was the place where we would most often find her. We have seen that she did not think of herself worthy to enter the chapel when she had asked to Mary Theresa Tegaiaguenta where the women and herself would be seated, because she believed to be the last person in the village.

I proposed that they should place her in the chapel after her death, because Our Lord had promised that His servants shall be where He is, and permits it for His glory. Father Cholenec had charge of the mission and judged it was not pertinent. We then placed her where her grave was made, where she had said three months before her death. Then four years later, we had her removed from the cemetery and brought her into the new church. She is the first to have this honour in this land. We had seen from experience that God approved of this honour that we have rendered to His servant.

Chapter 20

Catherine Tekakwitha had a tender devotion to the Mother of God from when she learned the qualities, the power, the glory of Our Lady and the method to honour Our Lady. We do not know how to explain the devotion she brought to the Mother of God when the Holy Family received her. She had marked the days of the week dedicated to the Blessed Virgin and on those days she carried out some penances or act of virtue. After she arrived from the Macquas, her instructress saw that she had some shell beads attached to the back of her hair. She asked Catherine if she was ready to leave these vanities in order to imitate the Blessed Virgin. Catherine obeyed at the first word and never wore them again. Catherine wanted to cut her hair to testify that she wanted to be forever at the service of the Virgin of Virgins, but the fear she had of being seen as virtuous was the reason she did not cut it. She was content with wearing her hair like the other modest girls of the village.

The virginity that Catherine always loved and always kept was the symbol of her attachment to having frequent devotions to the Blessed Virgin, which she had done with her body and life. She proposed Her life as a model and so that she could imitate Her as much as possible. This desire led her to make a procession, which I have mentioned, around her field in the snow and saying the Rosary several times without nearly ever leaving it. She had learned from her heart the Litanies of the Blessed Virgin. These she would say in privacy after the evening prayers in the cabin. She would say the Angelus with precision wherever she was, even in the forest, because it is a praiseworthy custom of the Natives from the Sault to say the Angelus three times a day.

Catherine wanted to imitate Saint Paul so that everyone could resemble her. Her manner of acting, her reputation and one that I do not know what the French and the Natives had observed in this young virgin Native girl, has done the miracle of our forests. She was motivation for several persons who wanted to learn from her what was most agreeable to God and to place into practice. Some of the things she did would make her hide, but sometimes she could not refuse instructions to others.

Virginity, chastity and continence were the balm that she spread everywhere. She had spoken of these virtues, which led others to embrace them and avoid vice while speaking of the Blessed Virgin, who was her refuge and model.

Two married people saw Catherine shortly after she had made her vow of perpetual virginity a little over a year before she died. The purpose of their visit was to learn from her the sort of life that a good Christian should lead in this world.

CATHERINE TEKAKWITHA: BOOK ONE

They knew the humility of Catherine would prevent her from speaking, so they sent for her companion to come to their cabin and at the same time they begged Catherine to come. The man was Francis Tsonnatouan and his wife was Margaret, who was no more than twenty-one years old and he slightly older. When Catherine and her companion entered, they closed the cabin door to testify that it was a great secret what they were asking to Catherine and one, which they were ready to have kept. Tsonnatouan began the discourse and addressed himself to Catherine and Mary Theresa. He said that he knew what they were doing and the life they had embraced. He said this to let them talk and then told them that he and his wife wanted to be good Christians and give themselves entirely to God. Catherine was very surprised at this and after some moments of silence told her companion to speak. They gave no advice to these two young married people other than to go to find and propose to the Father of their good intention.

He kept Catherine's portrait, some of her relics and also a little chaplet around his neck. He had called this little chaplet, the Chaplet of Catherine. The Chaplet of Catherine was composed of an Apostles' Creed that he said on the cross, a bead for the Our Father and another bead for the Hail Mary, and with three other shell beads for each a Glory Be to the Father.

This he had said in thanksgiving to the Blessed Trinity, for the graces bestowed to Catherine. He had always sustained the virtue of his wife, who was very devote and had from time to time dealt with her poverty with difficulty. He had a book of images depicting the Old and New Testaments and some other paintings too that he used for explaining the virtues and vices, the mysteries of the Rosary and many other mysteries. He exhorted more from example than from words and because of this he led many people to God, or more certainly Catherine gained them for him, because he felt obliged to her for whatever he had become, as compared with his previous life. Also, he had made himself a little chaplet from shell beads and marked his everyday acts of virtue, which he did during the morning and throughout the day. He merited from having his place in Catherine's life. This good Francis died in the month of April of this year 1695, and left his wife with an extraordinary devotion.

Chapter 21

A virtue that is so elevated can sometimes be a target for slander. The reputation held by Catherine was sometimes slandered in order to try her, but the demon would never receive fruit from her. She always remained patient, gentle and humble. After her death, she left her reputation in the hands of God, which He justified and exalted her to the highest degree of honour.

The trial was never more sensible than when she returned to the Sault from the winter hunt. She believed herself safe from the slanderous tongues, but when she was accused of a thing for which she was innocent, it deeply grieved her. A married woman and a good Christian, but somewhat prone to slander, had formed a very unfavourable judgement of Catherine on certain appearances only. One evening, her husband returned very tired from the hunt at a late hour because he had chased a moose all day. He entered the cabin after everyone was asleep and rested himself on the nearest place he found and went to sleep. The next morning, his wife had seen him asleep and looked to see the one next to him. She saw Catherine and unjustly judged her and her suspicion was confirmed by her husband. He had a canoe at the river and it needed sewing from some of the women, and as the time to leave was approaching, he asked Catherine to do it. Although these thoughts remained with this woman, and did not speak of them before returning to the village.

She had rather went to find Father Fremin, who had the charge of the mission, to tell him of her suspicions and the foundation of her judgement. The Father believed everything of this delicate matter from this woman who came to him. He spoke to Catherine to ask and advise her. Whatever Catherine might say, she was not entirely believed. Her instructress had spoken to Catherine again to bring remedy to the evil, if there was any, and to prevent it.

The good Catherine Tekakwitha would never suffer as much as on this occasion. What hurt her most was the Father did not seem to believe her, but instead accused her as if she was guilty. God had permitted this to prove her virtue, because there remained nothing more to a girl so virtuous after having left her country, her relatives and all of the conveniences she might have found in a good marriage. She was left with no desire but to practice abnegation in His honour and have nothing to accept from this century. This passed within her in an eminent degree. God had spoken and the admirable things passing after her death were reflected on those who were with her in the forest. They retracted their slanderous tongues of her conduct and were the first to praise her.

It is true that before drunkenness became prevalent among the Iroquois, there had been people among them who had the reputation of being chaste, because the vice of impurity was less common and marriages were better among the Iroquois than other Native nations. However, what the faith brought in Catherine had never been seen. Her modesty was depicted on her face and chastity seemed to be born with her.

One day, a young man passed by her cabin and saw Catherine sitting quite near to her instructress. He said laughingly, "They say the one there has sore eyes." At the same time, he had taken the end of her blanket and uncovered her face. It was with this act that he made her blush, but without becoming angry, she had gathered her blanket and listened with patience her mother, who was instructing her. Her enduring patience had made her invulnerable and incapable of hurting charity or of complaining about anyone and this was well seen in all that I have said of her.

She had said only what was necessary to let the truth be known, but never said anything to be seen that she was displeased with any of those who passed the winter with her during hunt. This argument alone is enough to silence those who they had a wrong opinion of her. The good reputation of the husband of the woman who had brought the accusation was one of the oldest Christians in the village for more than twenty years after his baptism. He had never given the occasion for someone to say ill of him and lived in content with his wife. In this manner, God had guided Catherine from a very thorny road. The actual thorns that she had served for her penance were only a symbol of the interior thorns that tormented her soul.

Chapter 22

Although the life of Catherine Tekakwitha had been one continual illness from her earliest years, she did not consider the discomforts of her eyesight that she experienced from the age of four. During the last year of her life, she had nearly continual headaches and a stomach illness, which were accompanied by vomiting and finally with a slow fever. She had the desire to learn to serve God at the Sault and the heavenly consolations of God fulfilled her. These sometimes diverted her thoughts entirely from her infirmities and with the assiduity with which she had at work would allow her to find the days very short. She had with all of this a smiling face and would appear as though she did not suffer at the height of her pains.

We always saw Catherine with her head covered during the middle of summer and while the other Native girls were very lightly clothed. Her instructress asked her the reason of this because it made her ill and took away the innocent comforts that the others take of themselves. Catherine replied that she would seem prideful if they saw her with her head lifted and not covered with her blanket or veil. She made a virtue of what she likely had to do, which was to cover her eyes from the very strong light of the sun. In this manner, her soul was so attached to God and profited from the least things. She would sanctify what would be uninteresting to another person. She hid herself when the people at the Sault began to know her as a Sister, and some of the French from La Prairie had a particular knowledge of her because they witnessed her modesty and religious reverence.

Chapter 23

God took Catherine from this the world when she began to be known to it. She had arrived at the Sault in the autumn of 1677 and passed a winter in the forest at the hunt. She had practiced extraordinary penance during the summer of 1679. She had taken the resolution not to go to the hunt any more, so she passed the winters in the village like the others who stay as a necessity. They only have corn to eat without meat. She would deprive herself of all the other conveniences like those who went to the hunt. She wanted the spiritual riches accorded to those who stay in the village during the winter. These were the holy masses that they were able to hear, the communions, the indulgences they could gain, instructions they have in the chapel and in the cabins, and the spirit of Christianity they could obtain more easily. In particular, Catherine was obliged to stay in the village because of the incident that happened to her the first winter when she was unjustly accused.

Also, we could say that God did not want her to die in the forest, where we would have been deprived of her great example of virtue, which she gave to the entire village in her death. It was on Wednesday, April 17, 1680, Catherine left this earth to enter heaven. After her death, I have been in a continual paradise with her and I have recommended myself to the prayers of this servant of God.

Her afflictions were increasing everyday nearing the end of 1679. Sometimes we saw her standing, although she was not able to leave her cabin. When she could go out, it was her pleasure to be in the chapel for part of the day either kneeling or resting on the benches when she could not support herself. If she had remained in the cabin alone, as often happened to the sick while the others are occupied in the fields, she would commune with God. In truth, she had never lost sight of Him by either mediating or saying her Rosary.

When I would visit her, she thought more of her soul than of her pains and her body, and she had never wanted me to leave her cabin. I had sometimes brought to her cabin the little children whom I was in the care of. This was to divert the thought of her pains, so that she could be contented and to teach her. To have a larger part of this instruction, Catherine had tried to raise herself, as weak as she was, to see the images that I described of the Old and New Testaments. The thanks and insistencies that Catherine had given in obliging me to return soon were the signs of the hunger and thirst she had of justice. However, she was so ill that a few days later she would die in odour of sanctity.

Chapter 24

Catherine Tekakwitha was blessed, because Our Lord had found her in a continual vigil. When the Holy Viaticum was given to her, we lost hope of seeing her healthy. It was Holy Week, and thus she obliged herself in memory of the Passion of Our Lord to demand that we accord her to engage in some penances. This was, for example, to pass a day without taking food and to fast. God had accepted her good intention. Instead of granting what she demanded, she was told that she must think of something else, because she did not have long to live. Who could say the joy she felt, especially when she was told that she was having the Body of Our Lord brought to her.

It was unprecedented in the village to see the Blessed Sacrament carried to a cabin, for the sick were brought on a board of bark to the chapel so as to have inspired the Natives with respect of the Blessed Sacrament. The Natives do not

CATHERINE TEKAKWITHA: BOOK ONE

consider themselves worthy enough to have Our Lord go to search for them. When it was necessary to give the Holy Viaticum to Catherine, it was found she was too weak to be moved and we had a great scruple to allow her to die without receiving this sacrament. Then the Holy Viaticum was brought to her without anyone finding fault, because she had merited more consideration than the others.

Catherine had gathered all her strength to properly make this last Holy Communion. She had begged her companion not to abandon her in this last moment. Catherine testified of her poverty, because it was so great that she had nothing to cover her modestly for this Holy Communion. Then her companion, knowing of it, lent her vest to Catherine. This extraordinary ceremony of having seen the Blessed Sacrament carried to a sick person, along with seeing the death of a saint, attracted everyone in the village. When Father Cholenec had entered and heard her Confession, Catherine renewed the offering to God that she made of her body and renounced again all the vanities. She had remembered all the graces received from God, especially those He bestowed on her from the time of her baptism, but most of all to have preserved the integrity of her body, which she had rendered very chaste to Him. We could then see the esteem that they had held of her virtues.

There were few people in the village, as most of them were still at the hunt, and those staying in the village continually came to visit her or recommended themselves to her prayers. Father Cholenec profited from this moment to oblige Catherine to influence those who needed encouragement in virtue. We had remarked that one way God inspires faith into the mission, which was to gain the healthy through the sick and especially from those about to die. The exhortations of the dying had often converted some who were previously not willing to be baptized or to confess, but we had never seen anything like what happened upon the death of Catherine. We saw the little she had talked during the two years when she was in the village, and she had made them enter into a new fervour. She was obliged against her inclinations to speak to certain devout people in particular and in general.

She employed the little time she had left from after her Last Communion or Holy Viaticum to her Extreme Unction in this exercise of charity and in continual acts of the love of Jesus. When everyone had pressed Father Cholenec to give Catherine the Extreme Unction, the Father ran all the way to the chapel to get the needed articles and blamed himself for having delayed it for such a long time. Catherine comforted them and said that there was enough time. The manner in which she said this to her companion made Father Cholenec and to several others believe that she had a revelation of the hour of her death.

Chapter 25

The morning of Holy Wednesday, Catherine's illness began to worsen. Her companion believed that she was about to give up her soul. She remained next to Catherine and was not able to leave. Although Catherine assured her companion to go to work in her field and promised to send for when it was time. It happened like had Catherine promised. She sent for her companion at about ten o'clock in the morning. Mary Theresa Tegaiaguenta arrived at her cabin a short time before Extreme Unction was given. After receiving the sacrament, Catherine talked with her companion.

However, she was constantly worsening. Father Cholenec was kneeling near her to say the Recommendations of the Soul to God, which are the last prayers of the dying, and heard a little of what Catherine was saying. He kept his eyes rested on her face to see what was happening and even encouraged them to continue speaking. Catherine had her face turned to heaven. Her companion had embraced her with one hand and supporting her cheek with the other while listening with attention to Catherine's last words. Then having difficulty in speaking by not being able to raise her voice and seeing her companion with tears, Catherine said her last parting salutation to her. Catherine said, "I am to leave you. I am going to die, remember always of what we have done together from when we have known of each other. If you change, I will accuse you before the tribunal of God. Take courage, despise the discourse of those who have no faith when they want to persuade you to marry, listen only to the Fathers. If you cannot serve God here, go to the Mission of Loreto. Never give up mortification. I will love you in heaven, I will pray for you, I will aid you." After these last words, this blessed girl lost her words when phlegm began to fall and would later take her away.

Then her eyes were closed for a long time. She could hear well until her very last breath well. Several times when some act was suggested to her, which she took new strength. When we exhorted her to the love of God, the expression of her face changed. And everyone wanted to take part at the devotion that her dying face had inspired. It had appeared more like the face of one in contemplation than of dying. She had remained as such until her last breath. Her respiration diminished continually for about nine to ten hours before her death and at the end became nearly imperceptible, but her face did not change. Father Cholenec was kneeling at her right side and he saw only a slight contraction of the nerve at that side of her mouth. She had died, it was as if she was falling asleep, which we were not certain of for a long time of her death. When we were assured of her death, we delivered her eulogy in her cabin to encourage everyone to imitate her. What was said from Father Cholenec and with what we saw, we regarded her body as a precious relic.

The simplicity of the Natives had made them do on this occasion more than was required. This was the kissing of her hands and keeping of her belongings as relics. They passed Wednesday evening and the rest of the night near her to admire her face, which had changed gradually in less than a quarter of an hour after her death. Her face gave devotion even though her soul was separated from her. Her face appeared more beautiful than when she had been living. This gave joy and strengthened everyone in the faith that they had embraced. It was a new argument of credibility to which God had favoured the Natives in order to make them witness the faith.

Chapter 26

The custom of the Natives was not to make a great preparation for a funeral. They would grease the hair and the faces of their dead and would sometimes dress them and with new moccasins or sometimes would only cover them.

A Frenchman in the village wanted to make her a coffin out of devotion to her. They placed her body in an ordinary manner, but it could not be possible to have covered her face when we placed her in the coffin because of the pleasure we had taken of looking at her face. This is why we left her face uncovered until she was buried. We read on this body what was said of her, which was an image of chastity and virginity. We had never said as much as in the catechisms that they have learned then. Her funeral was a day of both mourning and rejoicing. We were in mourning of her having left us, but we were rejoiced of having her as the Guardian Angel of the Sault.

Chapter 27

Father Jacques de Lamberville, who had baptized Catherine, said she was a treasure in his letter. Although he now added that he should have said something more about her.

Father Fremin said sometimes that this girl was a disgrace to those older Christians and the French, because he had seen such a virtue in Catherine and permitted her to be placed among the Holy Family as soon as she arrived from the Iroquois.

Father Cholenec gave her the Last Sacraments and praised her highly after she died.

I was present and had a particular confidence in her prayers. I have prayed an Our Father, a Hail Mary and three times the Glory Be to the Father at her grave from the very day of her burial. This is a devotion practiced among the Natives and the French, who go to Catherine's tomb when they want to receive favours from God.

In his journal, Father Francis Xavier de Charlevoix said of Catherine Tekakwitha, "In this manner, New France and like the capital of Old France, which sees appearing forth a poor Native girl and shepherdess with glory above so many apostolic men, martyrs and other saints of all conditions."

After a Jesuit Missionary amongst them was cured through her intercession, the Jesuit Fathers from the Islands of America recommended themselves to her in their prayers.

All the missionary Fathers passing at the Sault admired this marvel, and admitted the spirit of God guided her.

Father Louis de Maizerets, who was the Superior of the Seminary of Quebec, praised her during a visit and had said that she was the apostle of the Natives.

At his first visit to the Sault, Bishop Jean-Baptiste de Saint-Vallier came from Quebec with then-Governor of New France, Jacques-Rene de Brisay de Denonville. The Bishop prayed at the tomb of the Genevieve of New France, as he called Catherine.

Father Pierre Remy, of the Holy Angels Chapel in Lachine, frequently asks for her intercession and has his parishioners do the same and he also often calls Catherine Tekakwitha a saint.

Father Louis Geoffroy, who is the Pastor from La Prairie de la Madeleine, witnessed the marvels that Catherine had performed in his Parish and is ready to publish them everywhere.

Father Pierre-Joseph-Marie Chaumonot, having heard of the fall of the chapel at the Sault while the three Jesuit Fathers were in it, attributed the preservation of these Fathers from injury to the prayers of Catherine and recommended himself to her prayers.

Father Joseph de la Colombiere, Canon of the Cathedral of Quebec, had come especially to render his thanks at the tomb of Catherine, who had cured him.

The Natives and the French ask for her intercession in their necessities.

Finally, all of New France has commenced to be witness of her power next to God in 1695, fifteen years after her death, from the many cures she had done at Montreal and elsewhere. The harvest is large when we give saints to paradise.

Chapter 28

We cannot enough admire the spirit of a Native and young girl who had faith in our mysteries and was as lively as Catherine. Although she lived only four years after the time she had known the faith. Her devotion to the Blessed Sacrament and other practices was sufficient enough to prove this truth. She had a good and agile spirit. She learned her prayers in a short time and made her profession of faith without fear. In her longhouse, she was the only one baptized. She did not renounce her faith even though she was not well treated, because she had wanted to resemble the Natives of the Sault and was sometimes pointed out as a sorceress.

It was said that she had a certain promise, which held the revelation of her eternal happiness. We were astonished how very easily she promised prayers at the hour of her death, which she had not wanted to do during her life, because saying she was too young in Christianity to be praying to God for the others.

Catherine Tekakwitha had consumed her life from repeating three times these words, "Jesus, I love you." This love gave her strength in her illness, work and harsh penance, which she gave herself and finally when she had done an entire sacrifice with only a few hours to live. We often said that she never lost sight of God, especially in the forest, where she would compensate for the exterior graces said in the village and not in the forest. This we had said of her from admiration, and we could not understand that she could be so attached to Jesus.

The vice of slander was never known to her and those who knew her that they could not reproach her of anything. She was blessed with charity, and because of this everyone loved her. Although when slander twice attacked her and she could have complained of the others, she talked nothing further about those who had unjustly accused her.

She had appeared eminent in the various temptations when she found herself offending God, and was always well preserved even though when she lived for two years in her country in continual danger of offending God. Catherine was seen to have a good sense in her small exhortations. She was prudent, even in her excesses, which she went to excess to preserve the course that the Father had taught her.

I will not attempt to recount here at length all her virtues, because the work would be far too extensive. We could judge her other virtues from those seen here. She had an advantage to love religion, whereas others did not have this for the most part. Even before her baptism, she had a solid spirit and was not attached to dreams. She had the respect for all the ceremonies of the Church and everything regarding

Christianity was evidence of the esteem, which she had for her religion.

Her devotion was constant and never capricious and was also never falsely assumed. It was very difficult for her to have her body assist with her desires because of her infirmities. She would spend very long hours in the chapel kneeling and would rarely support herself when she was weak. If she remained in her cabin alone, she would commune with her Spouse or say the Rosary. She had often repeated, "Who will teach me what is most agreeable to God, so I could do it?" She was exact in all the practices of devotion, either small or of greater importance that were established in the mission. She had particular practices of devotions, which we saw and the promptness in leaving everything when the bell was rung for the prayers.

Her penances were admirable, although she was always exempt from great sins. She was such a great penitent like we had all known throughout her life. Her confessors were Father Cholenec and myself. We had testified, which she was an angel and her companion could not enough admire a conscience so pure as that of Catherine, who did not know what she had done against the law of God either before or after her baptism. The hatred of sin in which she had not fallen, or perhaps into which she feared to fall, was the cause of all her excess of penance. She so importuned Our Lord to take her from this corrupt world. She had died in the flower of her age and could not live with a body soaked in the waters of penance. She traced the way to heaven to the young Native girls, who did not want to succumb to temptations.

Her chastity was the most beautiful flower in her crown. It is a sort of miracle that she had escaped the deluge of impurity. Everyone, God and her conscience, had rendered testimony to the truth that Catherine never committed a sin of the flesh. God made the first cure of the sick that was in confirmation to the chastity of Catherine. She possessed chastity and of which she made the vow, because she had the merited. Father Cholenec had granted her this pious request and this solemn promise to God was pronounced before him. The experience of two inhabitants from La Prairie and two others from Lachine made them see the power she had to preserve people from the demon of impurity.

The sacrament of Confirmation was not administered to her. The Bishop gives Confirmation and the only Bishop of New France then resided in Quebec. It is a sacrament where we receive the Holy Spirit, which gives the strength to confess our faith without fear and lead a holy life despite the obstacles that provoke the demon. She had given proof of this since her baptism. Thus, we relieved her from sin as that of negligence by not having been confirmed.

The Father Superior of the Jesuit Society of New France admitted sometime before to refusing Catherine the honours owed to her because he felt as though there were illusions in her conduct and penance, but after having a complete examination, he had changed his thoughts.

Her instructress and I having admitted the same doubts and we prayed to God without communicating to each other, because we wanted to what to think of Catherine and her purity. After seeing two very remarkable appearances of her in the week following her death, we changed our sentiments, especially when we communicated between us some years later the lights we saw from above.

We say masses to thank God for the graces we receive everyday through her intercession. Pilgrimages are continually made to her tomb and the Natives followed her example.

They have become better Christians than they were before. Congregations are being found between them, especially among young girls with the objective of mutually assisting one another to live as Christians and to prepare themselves for the most heroic actions.

The earth had lost and heaven had gained, and the mission gave to paradise the blessed soul of Catherine Tekakwitha, a treasure sent to them two years previously. She died on Holy Wednesday, the seventeenth of April, 1680. The esteem she held during her life, the aid she bestowed upon many people after her death, the honours they have continued to render her and various other circumstances that adorned her life, have made her very well known throughout this country.

Catherine Tekakwitha had served the mission from her good example, but we can say that she served the mission more after her death. Her lifeless body is serving here as a testament to the Natives that faith is worthy of belief. Catherine's prayers continue to aid this mission.

BOOK TWO

†

THE LIFE OF CATHERINE TEKAKWITHA, FIRST IROQUOIS VIRGIN

by
Pierre Cholenec, S.J.

Chapter 1

Catherine Tekakwitha is the name of the sainted young woman, who I am going to write about. She is today so renowned in New France because of the extraordinary marvels that God has performed and continues to perform everywhere through her intercession. She was born in Caughnawaga, which was a settlement of the lower Iroquois among the Iroquois, in the year 1656. Her mother was from the Algonquin nation. She was baptized and raised among the French at Three Rivers. It was there that the Iroquois had taken her from the war with the French and brought as a slave to their country. She lived among them and soon after was married to one of the Chiefs of the village. She had two children, a boy and girl. The girl was called Tekakwitha.

It has been told that this virtuous woman preserved her faith and the fear of God during her captivity prayed until her last breath, but she did not have the time and consolation to inspire these praiseworthy sentiments in her two children. She had the joy of bringing them into the world and the sorrow of leaving it without seeing her desire of having them baptized. Smallpox had come among the Iroquois and a great many of them died from it. She succumbed to this common misfortune and left her two children, who were still very young and not capable of taking care of themselves.

She had prayed to Him, who was their Creator, so He could also be their Father and take them under His divine protection. We saw in Tekakwitha that God had heard such a prayer. Her brother had died from the same illness a little while after his mother. Tekakwitha also caught this disease, but Our Lord had chosen her to one day be His bride and saved her from death, so that in her the marvels of His grace might shine forth. She had remained very weak for the rest of her life. The smallpox affected her eyes and because of this, she was not able to endure the great light of the day. During her entire life she was forced to cover her head with a blanket when she left her longhouse, and this is how she is depicted in images. This was unlike the other Native girls, who would wear blankets on their shoulders. We do not know of the destiny of her father, but we know only that Tekakwitha was an orphan at the age of four and lived with her uncle, who was one of the most considered elders of the village. Her aunts had taken all the more care of her, because they had hoped to benefit from her in the future and succeeded in giving her a good education.

The child had a strong good disposition. She was of great gentleness and grew visibly in wisdom; and all her inclinations led to virtue. God wanted her for Himself. He had inspired her early with the love of work and of solitude. It could be said that these two inclinations were the sources of the innocent life, which she led in the country of the Iroquois.

When she was a little older, she was always at work in her longhouse. She gave her aunt all the services that she was capable of doing. She went out in public only when she had something to accomplish. She was always occupied in her longhouse, where she spent some of the time making little articles with extraordinary skill she possessed. She grinded the corn, went in search of water and carried wood, because these were the ordinary work of her gender among the Iroquois. She avoided idleness, which is so common among the girls and the source of infinite vices. She would avoid visiting other girls, as was the custom of the young Iroquois girls. What was still more admirable in her was the natural horror of all that was against purity. This horror had her leave any sort of gathering or assembly and led her to avoid dressing as the other Native girls, because of her sight.

She had allowed herself to be led from her aunts and with the only purpose of obeying and pleasing them. After she would regard this compliance as one of the greatest sins of her life, and she made of it a motive for shame and repented it with tears. This same horror of impurity and the love that she felt inside of her for chastity, without then knowing its merit, had made her refuse marriage when she was of a marriageable age. This young Iroquois had inclinations very much opposed to the purposes of her aunts. When her aunts wanted to oblige her to marry, she would excuse herself by affirming above all of her extreme youth and her little inclination to enter into marriage. The aunts seemed to approve of these reasons, but later they resolved again to betroth her when she least expected. It was not to allow her a choice of the person to whom she was to be united. Accordingly, they cast their eyes upon a young man whose alliance appeared desirable, and they had made the proposition to him and the members of his family. The matter had been settled on the two sides and in the evening the young man entered the longhouse and seated near her. Tekakwitha appeared disconcerted when she saw the young man seated next to her side. Then rising abruptly, she had left the longhouse without returning until the young man left.

This firmness outraged her relatives and she was to compensate dearly for what she had done because her aunts had looked upon this as an unbearable stubbornness that was inconceivable among the Iroquois. From this time, she had a great deal to suffer in her longhouse, where she was no longer looked upon as a child of the longhouse, but as a mistreated slave that had refused and was thus treated with severity at every opportunity. However, she behaved with such patience and of such gentleness in the midst of these rejections and bad treatments, because she had respect for her aunts in all other matters and she soon regained their affection. They had spoken no more to her of marriage and let her live in peace in her own way without troubling her any further.

Tekakwitha had always resisted with great determination and from a particular grace of Our Lord, which He without any doubt watched over the purity of His future spouse. God had turned this small persecution to good for His faithful servant and prepared her to receive Holy Baptism. This was the greatest of all graces and the only thing absent to have made her a holy girl, and to give the final perfection for the many natural good qualities that shone forth in her.

Chapter 2

In 1674, Father Jacques de Lamberville came to the village of Caughnawaga and was given the charge of the Chapel of Saint Peter. Tekakwitha had not heard of his instructions and felt a great desire to become a Christian. However, she was kept back, perhaps due to fear of her uncle, who joined in the opposition to the Christians, or due to modesty itself that made her too timid to disclose her sentiments to the Father. God had seen to it, which she had the means of satisfying her desire when she least thought of it.

It was autumn of 1675, and most of the women were in the fields for the harvest of the corn. Tekakwitha had received an injury in the foot and thus stayed in the village. Her aunts entrusted her with the care of the longhouse and all the domestic affairs while they were in the fields. She would spend the days in solitude. The Father had chosen this time to go to visit the longhouses and instruct to his leisure those who remained in the longhouses. One day, when making these afternoon customary visits to the longhouses and having already passed hers, because he believed no one to be there, he had felt an inspiration to turn back and enter.

The Father was most edified by her modesty and by her timid nature, but he was even more so when he had spoken with her and had learned what a virtuous life she led. He had spoken to her of Christianity and because he found her so docile, he pressed her to be instructed and to attend the chapel. She was overjoyed, because she had found her long desired occasion for embracing the Christian faith. After she recovered from her injury, she had conducted with assiduity her attendance at the chapel.

When he found her so faithful, he inquired about her conduct in her longhouse and everyone spoke well of her. In truth, he saw that she had none of the vices of the girls of her age and this encouraged him to instruct her regularly. The Father saw clearly that the Holy Spirit had enlightened the eyes of her soul to see the truth of our religion and to touch her heart to embrace it. After his first conversion with Tekakwitha, he believed that God had a great intention for this girl and because of this, he had resolved and promised to grant her the grace of being baptized of which she ardently desired.

After passing the entire winter in having taught her the prayers, teaching her thoroughly and preparing her to receive this sacrament, the Father appointed a day to be baptized. Father de Lamberville had foreseen that the great profits of his new Church might bring from baptism of a girl of her character. He wanted to confer it solemnly on the feast of the Resurrection, Sunday April 5, 1676. This was the most splendid day of the year. On this great day, he baptized her in the presence of all the Christians from the village. He assembled them so as to render the ceremony more impressive. Tekakwitha knelt while surrounded with catechumens and the newly converted. She listened to the Father instructing her of the importance of the occasion. After the usual inquiries and prayers, he conferred on her baptism.

He baptized her with the name of Catherine. Although a name already consecrated from the purity of many holy virgins, and to which one may say she gave a new lustre. Then everyone had witnessed the modesty and devotion, which she showed during the ceremony and they made evident the great joy they had in this baptism. They considered themselves fortunate for having among their small numbers such a person who was perfect and greatly admired in the village. They did not only hope from her piety, which she would adorn the religion that she had just embraced, but she would have many others follow her example. It did not take a long time to see that they were justified in the favourable opinion that everyone had formed in regard to this matter. Catherine had not only justified their hope, but also surpassed it due to the fervour she showed after baptism and one had reason to believe that the Holy Spirit filled her soul with His grace. A soul disposed to receive it from an innocence of life and could be said was angelic.

All these beautiful virtuous dispositions shone forth as soon as she was obliged to appear in public and assist at the common exercises of piety with those recent converts. She was confined to her longhouse until then. Her own character was perfect from the beginning, which she soon surpassed everyone. In less than a few months, she became to her companions a model of humility, devotion, sweetness, charity and all of the other Christian virtues. If one had respected her in the beginning, this same person would have soon felt admiration of a virtue from her, as she was so young and already so solid. In this manner, some months passed very peacefully.

In the beginning, even her relatives did not seem to disapprove of the new course of life that she was leading. The Holy Spirit has made us aware through the mouth of Wisdom that when the faithful soul begins to unite itself to God, this soul should prepare for temptation. This was proved to be true in Catherine's instance. Her extraordinary virtue brought upon her the persecutions even from those who had once admired her. They looked upon her life as so pure, but being a tacit reproach to their own manner of living. They had the intention of harming her reputation and attempted through several deceptions to taint her purity.

Catherine's confidence in God, the distrust she felt of herself, her faithfulness in prayer and the consideration for the feelings of others all made her fear even the shadow of sin and gave her a perfect victory over the enemies of her innocence. The exactness with which she showed on the feast days at the chapel was the cause of another storm. This had come upon her on the part of her relatives.

They had taken ill to her remaining in her longhouse, because on these particular days Catherine abstained from going to work with the others in the field. After a while, they came with unpleasant words and cast upon her the accusation that Christianity had made her effeminate and accustomed her to an indolent life. They did not even allow her anything to eat and oblige her through means of famine, because they wanted her to follow her relatives and to aid them in their labour. Catherine had endured their reproach and contempt with faithfulness. She preferred in those days to do without nourishment, which was not to have violated the law requiring the observance of the feast days and the ordinary practices of piety. This firmness could not be changed and would trouble her relatives more and more.

Whenever she went to the chapel, they caused her to be followed with showers of stones cast from drunken people or those that feigned to be. This extended even to the children, who had pointed their fingers at her and in derisive shouts called her the Christian. To avoid their insults, she was often obliged to take the most circuitous paths to the chapel.

One day when she returned to her longhouse, a young man entered abruptly with his raging eyes and a hatchet in his hand. He raised it as if to strike her and perhaps without any other purpose than to frighten her. Whatever might have been the intention of that Native, Catherine contented herself with modesty and bowed her head without showing the smallest emotion. This fearlessness was not expected and astonished the Native. Immediately, he left as if he was terrified by some invisible power. It was through these trials of patience and piety that Catherine had to spend the summer and autumn that followed her baptism.

The winter had brought her a little more tranquillity. She was not freed from suffering some crosses with one of her aunts. Her aunt was of a deceitful and menacing spirit. She could not endure the regular life of her niece. They had constantly condemned her and even with actions in the most indifferent words. It is a custom among the Natives for uncles to give the name of daughter to their nieces, who in turn would call their uncles with the name father. However, it happened once or twice that Catherine called the husband of her aunt by his proper name without any ill-intention. Her aunt's evil spirit needed nothing further as the foundation to cause a most atrocious calumny. This woman had pretended to believe that this manner of expression by Catherine was an evidence of an intimacy.

She went to search the missionary to accuse her and place an end in his mind for the sentiments of esteem he always had of Catherine. Father de Lamberville understood the evil spirit of this sort and learned what had given occasion to this hateful suspicion. He gave her a severe rebuke and sent her away completely confounded. Later, he had mentioned it to Catherine, who showed her absence of all falsehood when she replied with openness and confidence. Catherine declared from the kindness of Our Lord. She could not remember if she even stained the purity of herself and would not fear receiving any reproach on this view in the day of judgement. It was on this occasion that she had declared it, and perhaps we should not have known of this if she had not been placed on trial.

Chapter 3

After she was baptized, Catherine had remained a year and a half in her country. Father de Lamberville greatly admired her, because she had always showed the zeal and everyday was making new progress in virtue. This was the reason that he had wanted to transplant this flower to better soil, where it could take root surely and be away from the danger of corruption.

The Mission of Saint Francis Xavier existed for some years among the French at La Prairie de la Madeleine, where it was opposite to the island of Montreal. It was only a year before she came when it changed from this place to the foot of the Sault Saint Louis, from which it had obtained its name. We were at peace with the Iroquois at the time, and because of this peace, many of them came to this place. They came for the restfulness that could be enjoyed in it and they were soon baptized. They had followed the example of several

Huron families already established there. These fervent Christians had led such an edifying life that it was even witnessed by the French. This mission was a living image of the primitive Church.

The Iroquois came to the mission and when they had returned, they were of the many who speak publicly with praise of the marvels witnessed at the Sault. This became the only subject of conversion among the Iroquois. This place received a great number of those who wanted to share in the happiness of their fellow countrymen, particularly from among the Macquas.

On the very day Catherine had received baptism, which the Great Macqua came back to the mission with thirty Iroquois that he had gained for Jesus Christ. She would very willingly follow him, but she depended as I have said before on her uncle. He looked only with sorrow on the depopulation of his village and openly declared himself an enemy of those who thought of going to live among the French. It was there that Father de Lamberville thought God wanted to see Catherine.

He had sometimes spoken of this to her, especially when she came to mention to him the displeasure showed to her by those of her longhouse. To console her, he would say to her of the peace the Christians lived at the Sault Saint Francis Xavier. A peace, if she were there, she would find more gentleness in a day than she could enjoy in a year from remaining where she was. God would soon show her the way.

Catherine had an older sister from adoption who for some years been living at this mission with her husband. Her desire was to have Catherine share their happiness. She had her husband depart so that Catherine would be brought here and with him also went Ogeratarihen and a Native from the

Mission of Loreto. Her aunts seemed willing for her to go, but her uncle was to be feared because he was strongly opposed to these transmigrations that left his country to populate ours. However, heaven interfered for Catherine.

They reached the village where Catherine was living with difficulty. Her brother-in-law had informed her secretly of the object of his voyage. This was the desire of her sister so that she should be with her at the Mission of the Sault. He said this praise in a few words.

Ogeratarihen entered the cabin of the Father and there was at once a crowd of people as was the custom of the country. They came to greet this visitor and among them was Catherine. This man, seeing they had assembled before him, began to talk to them of Christianity and of the happiness experienced by those who came to live at Sault Saint Francis Xavier. Catherine was touched by those words as if God had addressed to her the words of this preacher. She sought and told the Father, she was determined to do what he had so often advised her. She had begged him earnestly to take proper measures to restrain her relatives, who wanted to prevent her from leaving.

He had placed her in the care of Ogeratarihen, who strongly confirmed Catherine in her resolution. At the time, her uncle was negotiating with the English at Fort Orange, and they had profited from this favourable circumstance to start their voyage. Catherine arrived in the autumn of 1677. This was with a treasure of merit to herself, splendid examples for us, to the glory of God and of the great profit of the mission, which she is a powerful protectress against its visible and invisible enemies.

Chapter 4

God had chosen Catherine Tekakwitha so that in her the marvels of His grace could shine forth. He had not allowed her to live any longer in a land that did not deserve to possess her. He had sent her to the Sault to fortify the mission in its early days and to edify it by the examples of an angelic life. Father Fremin, who was one of the great missionaries of New France, had the charge of the mission and with him were Father Chauchetiere and myself.

Catherine was directed to me from Father Jacques de Lamberville and the letter she had brought from him contained this message, "Catherine Tekakwitha will stay at the Sault. Will you take the charge, I beg you, of her direction? You will soon know the treasure that we have given you. Guard it well then! When in your hands, she will profit to the glory of God from the salvation of a soul that is, assuredly, very dear to Him." On this recommendation, Father Fremin wanted that me to take upon myself the care of her direction, because I already had the charge of the instruction given to the Natives for baptism, the Sacraments of Penance and of Holy Communion.

After having arrived at the Sault, Catherine went to live in the cabin of the family of her brother-in-law, who had brought her into the country. The cabin belonged to an old Christian, Anastasia Tegonhatsihongo, who was among the first of the Iroquois to be baptized by our Fathers. She was one of the pillars of the mission and a most fervent member of the Confraternity of the Holy Family. The entire village had known her as the best to instruct, and her only occupation was to prepare those of her own gender for baptism. This woman had known Catherine and her mother in their country when she was little. She began to aid Catherine greatly at the Sault in progressing with her virtues. She had taken the place of her mother and was her principal instructress, which are the two names that we will call her in the future.

If one has read attentively all that has been said, it is easy to conclude that Catherine lived among the Iroquois as in a country not her own, even though she had been born there. In truth, Catherine was born to be virtuous. On the contrary, the country of the Sault had seemed her native land. If God owed a virtuous girl to this mission, we could say that He owed to Catherine this holy mission, where for several years the Iroquois retired here to profess the Christian religion and to live with all the piety of a new Church. In truth, the mission was very fervent at that time and they spoke of God alone. They had thought only of serving Him and did not limit themselves to the mere obedience of the Commandments of God. They showed the practices of the Evangelical

Counsels and everyone was living a life of holiness. The youngest and the oldest were either trying to equal or surpass the other, and almost all the cabins were schools of virtue and holiness.

Catherine's eyes were struck with many beautiful things when she saw with pleasure these new converts. In her relatives and the others that came from the Iroquois she saw the change in their manner of living. She had admired the Christian life they led and it was very different from the one they led a short time ago in their country. She had compared what they were here with what they were there. She reflected gravely on their happiness. She felt an unbelievable joy after a fortunate exile and being happily transplanted here where she sought for such a long time without ever knowing what it was. She would speak of it to us with ecstasy. As she was of a big heart, noble, and haste of spirit and since as far as we were able to discover that she possessed and insatiable desire to learn what was good, and an equal ardour to put into practice what she had learned once. Her well-disposed soul had caught fire. She put to the work immediately and she began to practice the things she saw the others doing. She did them with such happiness and made such notable progress. Within less than a few weeks, she had distinguished herself among all the girls and women of the mission. She had soon gained the esteem and the admiration of everyone. Catherine Tekakwitha was kept for more than twenty years among the evil and the sinful. She became a saint here among the just and the faithful.

She was the most fervent of entire the village. She was quite infirm and nearly always ill, but she did astonishing things in these matters. It was astonishing to see how far this young girl advanced in piety during about the two and a half years that she had lived at the Sault. It is more astonishing still that she possessed such a virtue almost from the very beginning. In truth, she was never a novice in the exercise of virtue, but she was accomplished in it from the beginning and attained rapidly perfection, which she had the Holy Spirit as her teacher.

Chapter 5

Catherine was not content with an ordinary life. She was pressed from this insatiable desire for good and through her extreme fervour to accomplish more. She began to embrace what was most perfect. She had taken her principal and the only rule of conduct was to search for all things that would be most pleasing to God. She kept nothing from Him and to have a rule to give Him everything that depended on her without any return for herself. This holy rule of conduct had as its foundation the exalted idea that she was made in the likeness of God.

She was chosen among the many others left in darkness to see the Light of the Gospel and to understand the true meaning of the Mission of the Sault. God bestowed this great grace on her. She felt an extreme gratefulness for this grace and retained it during her life. She was inspired with such beautiful principles, strong and efficacious motives. The first thing this virtuous Native girl had done was to attach herself to the holy place that was the chapel. She had made the chapel her dearest and the most habitual refuge, because she was certain of always finding Him there as she had already consecrated her heart and of all her affections to Him.

She would go to the chapel every morning during the winter and the summer. This was to converse with Him far from all the noise and without any distractions from the others. She would go as early as four o'clock in the morning and also before the bell was rung everyday at that hour. She would be found in prayer at the door of the chapel even during the severest winter weather.

She was in the chapel praying and remained there for several hours in succession. In the summer, she would hear the first mass at five o'clock in the morning that is, at dawn when it was for those who were in greatest haste to go to work. She would hear the second mass for the Natives at half past five o'clock in the morning that was at sunrise, and in the winter, this mass was said at ten o'clock in the morning. She always seem as though she was lifted out of herself when she had prayed and communed with Our Lord. She returned often during the day and interrupted her work to satisfy her devotion. Finally, when her work was done, she returned again in the evening and left only late at night. She was the first in the morning to enter the chapel and last every night to leave.

This fervour that filled her in the chapel had shone forth even more in her prayers. She learned the prayers said in common with marvellous persevering effort. She prayed very little with her lips, but a great deal with her eyes and heart. Her eyes were always filled with tears while she sighed deeply from her heart.

She would appear not to move and closed herself within herself. While the rest were asleep, she continued her prayers into the night. Again she would begin to say her prayers much before dawn and after only a very short sleep. She had such an eagerness to unite herself to God in her prayers that she attained this union without any other teacher than the Holy Spirit. She had a sublime gift of prayer and together with such heavenly gentleness; she often passed several hours at a time communing with God. From this source, she had acquired the great virtues that we shall speak at the end.

Her devotion was all the more admirable because it was not one of those idle devotions where there is usually only admiration for oneself. Catherine was not an obstinate devotee who is in the chapel when she should be doing the work of the cabin. In attaching herself to God, she had attached herself to work and as to a very proper means of having been united with Him. She had kept during the entire day the good inspirations received in the morning at the foot of the altar. It was because of this that she formed a great friendship with the good Anastasia. She had made it a rule to avoid all others and to go with her alone, either to the forest or to the fields. They went together, because they had only one purpose. This was to search for their God, whom they offered their work. They would hold pious conversions between themselves while performing their tasks.

Anastasia would speak to Catherine only of God, the means of pleasing Him and advancing her in His service, the life and habits of the good Christians, the fervour of the saints and their hatred of sin and the harsh penance performed for the reparation of the sins they had committed. Catherine had sanctified her work from spiritual conferences. This conversation so holy and together with her zeal for the things of God would result in her always coming away with new desires to give herself entirely to Him and place into practice what she had just heard.

She found God everywhere, whether she was in the chapel, in the forest or in the fields, because she feared even living one moment not spent for Him. She was seen coming and going with a Rosary in her hand while reciting the Rosary many times over the course of the day. This led her instructress to say that Catherine never lost sight of her God and always walked in His presence.

If rain or extreme cold had prevented her from working, she passed almost all her time before the Blessed Sacrament. The weeks and days for her were truly holy weeks and holy days. This I may say, with the language of the Holy Scriptures, were weeks were filled with virtue and merit.

Chapter 6

In this manner, Catherine lived from the autumn she had arrived at the Sault until Christmas. During this time she led such a fervent and exemplary life. She merited at this time a grace not granted to those coming from the Iroquois; that is to say, who only would receive it after several years and after having passed through many trials. This was to give them a high idea of that grace and obliged them to render themselves worthy of a life of not meriting reproach. This was not so for Catherine. She was very well inclined to receive Our Lord and she also wanted with a great eagerness to receive Him. I promised her the permission she had such earnestly desired of this great grace. On approaching the feast of Christmas, Saturday December 25, 1677, she would receive her First Communion after she was instructed in the mystery.

She received the good news with all imaginable joy and prepared herself for this great event with an increase of devotion suitable to the exalted idea she had of it. However, it must be admitted it was at this First Communion that all her fervour was renewed. The ground was so well prepared and only the approach of this divine fire was necessary to receive all its warmth. She approached and surrendered herself to this furnace of sacred love that burns on our altars. For the first time in her life, she had received the Holy Eucharist, which was through a degree of fervour proportional to the reverence and sincerity she had for this grace. She had come away from it so glowing with its divine fire. Only Our Lord knew what had passed between Himself and His dear spouse during her First Communion. We could say that day on, she appeared different to us, because she remained so full of God and love of Him.

We did not have to be long in her company to feel surrounded with the fullness of God and His love as she was. All her joy was to have the thought of Our Lord and converse intimately with Him. This will seem much unexpected in a young Native, but it will seem even more when I add that after having the happiness of receiving Holy Communion frequently, she always did with the same disposition and fervour as at her First Communion. She had received the same love with many and diverse graces from Our Lord. He would search only to visit us in this Sacrament of Love. He places no limits to His grace when He comes in contact with hearts disposed to receive His graces. He would profit from these hearts, which was especially true with Catherine.

She passed almost every Sundays and Holy Days in the chapel from early morning at the ten o'clock mass until late at night. If she were to leave a little while for meals, she returned immediately at the foot of the altar and always on her knees. She was possessed with an odour of the divine presence and when communing with Jesus Christ. On working days, she often went to the chapel during the course of the day and offered her work. In the evening, she would return again to the chapel and did not leave the chapel until late at night. In truth, it cannot accurately be told how often she visited the Blessed Sacrament, how many long prayers she poured out before the altar and the abundance of tears with which she approached the Holy Table. In turn, the gratifications of the Spouse of virgins flooded her virgin soul.

When she was in prayer, she had seemed entirely unconscious of what was passing outside her. This truth was so well known in the village. At the time of general Communion, the most devout women hastened to place themselves near her in the chapel when she prayed. They claimed her appearance was so devotional and ardent that her example would inspire them. Her presence had served as an excellent preparation to approach the Holy Table in a proper manner.

Catherine always ended each week with an exact investigation of her faults and the imperfections that she might have. Then she had her sins taken away through the Sacrament of Penance, she went to Confession every Saturday evening or more often. She prepared her confessions in such an extraordinary manner that it could have been only inspired by the Holy Spirit. He was the first that gave her a love of suffering and we shall see later of her hatred of her body. When she had prepared herself for confessions, she began with the last part; that is, the penance. This generous girl would go into the forest and tear her shoulders open with willow shoots. Afterwards, she went to the chapel and passed an entire hour weeping and sighing while she would prepare for her Confession. When she would begin, and during her confessions, she interrupted her words with such loud sobs. It would have given her confessor a great deal of difficulty in understanding her if he had not otherwise known of her angelic innocence.

She thought of herself as the greatest sinner in the world. It was with this sentiment of humility that she had made all her confessions. The same fervour was especially evident every time she would receive Communion. She was sometimes asked, "Catherine, do you love Our Lord?" It was enough to see her immediately overcome, "Ah, my Father! Ah, my Father!" She would say and could say no more. Her desire was to be always united with God and not to be distracted by the others. This made her love solitude even more, but her desire was also to preserve herself in innocence from the horror of sin and the fear of displeasing God.

Chapter 7

After Christmas, it was time to go for the hunt. Catherine went with her sister and her brother-in-law. It was not to divert herself or the desire to feast that had Catherine go to the hunt, which are the reasons most of the women go. Instead, it was only to satisfy this good sister and her husband.

God wanted her to sanctify herself in the forest as she had done in the village. This was to prove to all the Natives through the beautiful example she gave that virtue could be practiced equally both of these places. She continued to exercise the piety that she had practiced in the village. She had supplemented for those she could not do there and from others that her devotion had suggested to her. Her time was as regulated as that of a Sister.

She prayed before dawn while the others were still asleep. Again, she prayed at dawn with the common prayers, according to the praiseworthy custom of the Natives, which is that they say together in the mornings and the evenings. She would continue her evening prayers late into the night while the others slept. After the morning prayers, Catherine retired to solitude to pray again at sunrise while the men ate and made their preparations for the hunt. She would unite in spirit the people of the village at about the same time the Natives heard mass at the mission. In the winter, this is said at a quarter to seven o'clock in the morning; that is to say, at sunrise.

She had united her soul with that of the Father and prayed to her Guardian Angel to be present for her and to bring her the fruit of the Holy Sacrifice. It was for this purpose that she made a small shrine on the side of a stream. The shrine consisted of a cross that she carved in the bark of a tree.

When she thought the men had departed to the hunt, she returned to the cabin and occupied herself there all day long in the manner of the other women. This was in gathering wood and bringing back the meat of the animals killed or making wampum belts in the cabin. During this latter occupation, she had always invited the others to sing some devotional hymns, or to say some things from the lives and narrations of the saints that she heard during the sermons at the chapel on Sundays and on feast days. She was often the first to begin these discourses to encourage them. She had two purposes in this: to avoid bad conversation and frivolous talk, because they would only distract the spirit; and to constantly preserve her fervour and union with God, which was as strong in the forest as it had been at the foot of the altar in the village. This was the reason that her principal occupation, and the one she had taken the most pleasure, was to gather wood for the cabin, because she could be alone and could satisfy her devotion and converse intimately with her divine Spouse. Her humility was working for the others. This was through acting as the servant of the cabin while being at the hunt. Her desire for suffering was through tiring her body with continued labour of a painful nature.

She found another mean of penance from a more spiritual and secret exercise. She would fast while there was an abundance of good meat. She would leave the cabin to gather wood before the sagamite was ready and would not return until evening. She would then eat very little and even though her extreme fatigue and natural weakness she would spend part of the night in prayer. If in the morning they would oblige her to eat before going to work, she would secretly mix ashes with the sagamite to take away any pleasure she might have and leave her nothing but the taste of bitterness. She had begun practice of mortification in the village whenever she was able to do without being seen.

She had never become so attached to work either in the forest or at the cabin, where she forgot her shrine during her stay in the forest. On the contrary, she had taken care to return there from time to time and satisfy the hunger of her soul while she would let her body fast. Throughout the winter hunt, she went there every morning, evening and several other times during the week. She would end her devotions through harsh self-chastisement with branches. She had undertaken this sort of penance in secret with the direction of the Holy Spirit alone.

The life for Catherine in the forest was most praiseworthy and even of great merit to herself, but she was not content there and this was easily seen through her endurance, as she was not in her own natural dwelling place. The chapel, the Blessed Sacrament, masses, benedictions, sermons and other similar devotions had given her much pleasure in the short time that she was at the Sault and held a strong charm for her. This constantly brought her closer to the village and attached her heart and all its affections to the village. If her body was in the forest, then her spirit was at the Sault. This temporary stay in the forest is generally so agreeable to those of her gender because they think only of having a pleasant time and amusing themselves by being far away from all the cares of their cabins, but this was a burden to her and soon she had felt a great aversion to her stay.

An incident took place while she was there. It completed her dislike of her stay. This incident, and combined with the other reasons mentioned, made her take the resolution never to return there once she got back to the mission. A man from the group had chased a moose for an entire day. He returned very late and tired to the cabin. He went to sleep at the first place he could find without taking any food or water. His wife awoke the next morning and did not find him near her, but she saw him asleep near the mat of Catherine. As the Natives are very suspicious, she thought that her husband sinned with this young girl. This woman confirmed her judgement by Catherine's comings and goings, when it has been said that Catherine went to the shrine to pray and do her ordinary penance.

After having weighed these appearances in her mind, this woman believed it was a long established relation between them. However, she had the discretion not to show her suspicion and speak of it to no one, as she was a virtuous and wise woman. She then told everything after her return from the hunt to Father Fremin, who had the charge of the mission.

CATHERINE TEKAKWITHA: BOOK TWO

In this manner, God on His elect has placed their virtue to trial from similar happenings and render their virtue perfect in the fires of tribulation, allowing it to be blackened from slander and hideous calumnies. In this matter, He had even permitted the missionary to not take the Catherine's side at the beginning. If on one hand, the horror of impurity of this chaste girl and her innocence of life that he did not ignore would make him judge that she was perhaps not guilty. On the other hand, the woman persuaded him that whom she was speaking of might not be that innocent. Having enlightened himself in this delicate matter, he decided to have Catherine herself come to him. The Father had such a good opinion of her and was sure of her great sincerity. He resolved not to disclose the matter, but to listen to what she would say and believe her own testimony. Then the Father spoke to her and disclosed to her what was said of her and asked her of the matter. Catherine was satisfied through merely denying what was wrongly said, without showing any emotion about it, because she knew she was absolutely innocent. This great tranquillity of soul in this matter would naturally be so sensitive to her justified her perfectly in the mind of the missionary, who had already decided in her favour. This was not the situation with the accuser and with a few others, who in some manner had known of the woman's suspicion.

God had allowed it to be; that is, to have augmented the crown and merit of His faithful servant, because she had left her relatives, her country and the advantages that she might have found in a good marriage. After having sacrificed all of these for Our Lord, it only remained to sacrifice her honour and reputation, which she had generously abandoned for Him on this occasion. She was content to see herself held in contempt and having being passed as a great sinner, because of this reason that she did not hasten to find out who had spoken badly of her and she allowed the matter to die away. Although as it concerned someone else, all the vengeance that she took was praying to God for them. However, God on His part had sufficiently rewarded Catherine of such heroic relinquishment and resignation after her death from this very place where she suffered. The marvels she began to cause after her death made those that formed such an unjust opinion of her examine themselves. As like the two disciples going to Emmaus with Our Lord had not recognized Him, when He had broken the bread their eyes were opened to the miracle of the Resurrection. They then condemned themselves for their disbelief and likewise it was with those who Catherine had hidden her virtue in the forest and in the village that readily defamed her before they had known the truth. When they were touched by all the marvels they heard after her death, they were the first to make known her virtues and to remember her modesty, gentleness, charity, patience, devotion and the beautiful example that she had given them. From that time forward they would remain very devoted to Catherine. The woman who was the cause of the entire affair spent three entire years crying for her mistake without being able to find consolation, because she thought that Our Lord would never forgive her for having wrongly accused such a saintly girl. It was necessary for the missionary to apply all the authority he had on her spirit in order to retrieve it from its error as well as from the pain and sorrow she had felt over it.

Chapter 8

Catherine, having returned to the village, thought only of repairing the graces she had lost while in the forest. She had begun again frequenting the chapel with her ordinary fervour and eagerness. She joined her instructress so as to profit from her pious exhortations during their work.

Easter Sunday was approaching and those who were not far from the village on the hunt returned to the mission according to their custom and celebrate the great day. It was the first time that Catherine had celebrated Easter Sunday with us and was of great good for her soul. She assisted at all the services of Holy Week, which she admired all their solemn ceremonies and received from them a new esteem for the religion.

She was so touched by the gentleness and the heavenly consolations. She shed many tears, especially on Good Friday during the sermon on the Passion of Our Lord. Her heart was melted at the thought of the suffering of Our Saviour and she thanked Him a thousand times. She adored and kissed His cross with feelings of the most tender gratefulness and ardent love. She attached herself to the cross that day with Him and taking the resolution to repeat on her virgin body the mortification of Jesus Christ for the rest of her days and as if she had done nothing until then.

On Easter Sunday April 10, 1678, she received Holy Communion for the second time and did so with the same disposition, fervour and fruits that she had on the Christmas day. Then having completed these benefits and spiritual graces, she received a second grace from the Father on that day, even though he accorded this grace very scarcely and proved the esteem he had of her virtue.

The Bishop Francis Montmorency de Laval, the first Bishop of Quebec and a Prelate full of zeal, had already established the devotion of the Holy Family in his Episcopal town as a very proper purpose to sanctify the Holy Family. This would cause a great amount of good among the families and still does constantly to the edification of the entire country. From Quebec, this devotion was spread to other parishes with the same results. In 1671, Father Fremin had the charge of the mission and believed it was proper to establish the devotion of the Holy Family because it was a good method of having maintained and increased the fervour of the new Church.

It was decided only to admit a few of the more fervent people of the two genders so as to give a higher perception of it and to oblige the members who were honoured by such a great grace to respond by the holiness of their lives. In this, they did not fail, because once the Natives give themselves to

CATHERINE TEKAKWITHA: BOOK TWO

God, they are capable of the greatest and most wholehearted devotion. The small number of chosen souls had raised its new character from an exemplary piety. Some were even so austere that the rest of the village looked upon them with a sort of veneration. To call a person a saint or a member of the Holy Family was to say one and the same thing. They kept this name as a particular sign in the mission.

Catherine was still very young and had only been at the Sault about seven or eight months. I had Father Fremin admitted her to this small number, where others were received only at an advanced age and after several years of probation. As we have already said, her virtue placed her above the rule for the ordinary people of the village. The members, far from being envious, had generally approved of her admittance. The members of the Holy Family had especially shown their joy and looked upon Catherine as capable of sustaining herself alone in this saintly community through her good examples. She was the only one who considered herself unworthy with the humble ideas that she had of herself. The more she had thought of her unworthiness, the more she thought of it as an obligation to work towards her perfection. So as not to lessen her fervour towards the devotion to the Holy Family, she gave a new exalted reputation. What is certain is the memory of her alone was sufficient to inspire, and still continues to inspire the fervour of many others.

She had advanced visibly and was profiting from everything that she acquired from motives and means. She was to grow in grace and holiness, because she grew more and more attached to Our Lord. In the opinion of Father Chauchetiere, she had already lived the life of union with God. In truth, she had tasted all the gentleness of that blessed condition before passing through the preparatory stages, which are the Purgative and Illuminative, with a particular guidance from the Holy Spirit. She entered against the ordinary manner in the preparatory stages by the third stage. This was the life of union with God. For the reason of having conducting herself with more merit and in a manner more excellent. In her intimate communications with God, she was filled with new inspirations of ardour and zeal. These at once had enlightened her understanding; that is, to make her see the beauty of the Christian virtues with reference to Jesus Christ, even though she always had Him before her eyes. These virtues had touched also her will to place them into practice and to conform herself as much as she could of, to become so perfect and at the same time to become so amiable. With these inspirations, she even went as far as to search her past for new motives of loving Him and hating herself.

She looked upon the smallest faults she committed as crimes and outrages against the divine Majesty while living among the Iroquois. She had chastised her body, which was so innocent and looking upon it as guilty. These faults were some of the principal reasons why she led such an austere life at the Sault, because it gave her a great thirst for mortification and suffering. Her instructress had contributed to this through speaking to her often of the pains of hell and the terrible penance the saints gave themselves to avoid these pains. The Iroquois Christians performed this because they had often offended Our Lord before becoming Christians.

She was further inspired by this because of an accident that happened to her at this time. This accident almost took her from among us when we were just beginning to know her. One day, she was cutting down a tree in the forest and it fell sooner than she had expected. Her hastiness saved her from being hit by the trunk, but one of the branches fell on her as she fled and hit her head with such a force that she lost her senses. At first, they thought she was dead, but she some time later revived and softly whispered, "Ah, Jesus! I thank you of having rescued me from this danger." The only conclusion she took from this was that God had saved her so that she could do penance for her sins. This she declared to her dear companion, who was such a great part in her life and of whom we must speak of now. She formed a part of the history that we are writing now about Catherine Tekakwitha.

Chapter 9

In the spring of 1678, God gave Catherine a companion, who aided her greatly in her progress and from whom we have learned several important things concerning Catherine. Her companion was the only one that had the confidence of Catherine, who communicated to her the most intimate thoughts and actions from the first day they met each other. It is true until then that Catherine never wanted to attach herself to anyone except the good Anastasia. She had taken the place of her mother and the frequent exhortations that she did as an instructress greatly aided Catherine in taking the right course of action that she was now pursuing. The good Anastasia was advanced in age and could not increase the fervour of her pupil, who had already surpassed her and was performing actions the older woman was not capable of.

CATHERINE TEKAKWITHA: BOOK TWO

Catherine needed a companion more of her own age. A companion that had the same resolution of giving herself entirely to God and was capable of leading the same sort of austere life that she had embraced. God allow her to find such a companion in the person of a young woman. She was baptized in her country by Father Bruyas. This woman, Mary Theresa Tegaiaguenta, had fallen into drunkenness after her baptism. The only thing Christian about her was her name. Even after she came with her family to live at La Prairie she was no better there at the beginning of her stay. She went to the hunt with her husband, who was not a Christian. Fortunately, she found there the cause of her conversion in an event that happened to her. I am going to relate here in a few words to see what means God had taken to convert this Native, who was to contribute so much to the Catherine's holiness.

She had departed at the beginning of the autumn with her husband and a young child, who was a son of her sister, to go hunting along the Outaouacs River. On the road, they were met by some other Iroquois who joined them and then they were eleven people: four men, four women and three children. Unfortunately, the snow fell very late that year so they were not able to hunt. After they had eaten their provisions with the meat from a moose her husband had killed, they were soon reduced to eat herbs because of the hunger.

Her husband had become sick and two men of the group, who were a Macqua and a Seneca, went hunting and intended to return at the very latest in ten days. The Macqua returned alone within the appointed time and assured them that his companion had died of hunger, but they suspected him of having killed his friend and lived on the flesh while he was away. They doubted him even more, because he was in such good health and admitted to killing no animal. They no longer hoped of securing anything from these hunters. They wanted to persuade the Christian woman to let her husband die and save herself, her nephew and all the others. She would not consent to it and she generously resisted it. They then abandoned her with her husband and nephew. Two days later, the sick man died. She regretted that he had not been baptized. After she buried her husband, she sought the road again carrying her nephew on her shoulders. After a few days, they had rejoined the group, who were searching the road to the Great River to go to La Prairie.

They were weak and exhausted after their twenty days of wandering and then they decided to take the resolution to kill one of the group so the rest would live. They had come upon the widow of the Seneca and his two children. They asked the Christian woman whether it was permissible to kill them and what the Christian law was on this view, because she was the only one of the group who had been baptized. She did not dare to answer this question, because she had not the sufficient knowledge to decide on the answer and for the fear she would contribute to the killing of someone. She had apprehended with reason that with her answer they would kill her too. Later, some of them killed the woman and her two children. Her eyes were opened to the danger to her body and she began to realize the deplorable condition of her soul was more miserable than of her body.

She had felt great horror due to her sins and the great fault in coming to the hunt without going to Confession. She asked that God grant her forgiveness from the bottom of her heart. She promised Him that if she was delivered from this danger and brought safely to the village, she would confess herself immediately and reform her life with prayer and penance.

God wanted this woman to have made Catherine known to her. She kept part of her promise and went to Confession on her return, but she placed aside for some time her life-reformation and the promised to do penance. This took place in the winter of 1675-1676. In autumn 1676, the mission was transferred from La Prairie de la Madeleine to the Sault Saint Louis.

Chapter 10

In the autumn of 1677, Catherine came to live there and in the following spring of 1678, she had become acquainted with her companion. The first chapel of the Sault was then under construction. One day, Catherine walked around this chapel, as did the Christian of whom we speak. It was merely to see how the work was progressing. God had planned this unexpected meeting for His glory and the good of these two souls.

It was here that they greeted and spoken to each other for the first time. Catherine asked where the women would sit in the chapel and her companion replied and showed where she thought their place would be. With a sigh, Catherine replied, "As it is true, it is not in this material temple God most loves to dwell. It is in us God wants to take up His dwelling place. Our souls are the temples most agreeable to God. But the miserable being I am, how many times having I forced God to abandon my soul in where God should reign alone! I deserve to be punished for my ingratitude and forever excluded from this temple here rising to His glory." These were the sentiments of profound humility, which were said with tears and words of grace. These words touched Mary Theresa, because she did not expect them and were to her words of life, grace and salvation. Mary Theresa was touched through remorse and soon resolved to fulfill the principal part of the promise that she had made while on the hunt.

Mary Theresa Tegaiaguenta was of a fiery temperament and went to extremes in good or evil. She was strong and strongly built in appearance and was in the prime of her life; that is to say, about twenty-eight or thirty years old. She gradually became enlightened while listening to Catherine and believing what she had said came from God. He sent this holy girl, who so much good was spoken of, to aid her in changing her life as had promised. Then she told Catherine of her ideas. They found their hearts and plans were in perfect harmony. They became friends during this first conversion and one word leading to another, they had then communicated their most secret thoughts to each other. To talk more easily, they seated themselves at the foot of a cross on the bank of the Great River that was near the chapel. They told each other of their past lives and resolved to unite themselves in penance.

They spoke to me of this union, because I was their spiritual director, and asked my approval. I happily gave them my approval seeing that it would be good for them. From this time, they become one in heart and soul and were inseparable until the death of Catherine, who after was always in the mind of her companion. Catherine did not neglect Anastasia and still occasionally visited her, but Catherine had devoted herself entirely to this second companion, who was more zealous and able to aid her more in her devotions.

They could be seen going to the forest, the fields and everywhere together. They would avoid meeting with other girls and women. This they did to avoid the unimportant matters of the village and not to cause to turn themselves aside from their devotions. They would speak only of God and the things pertaining to Him. Their conversations were like many spiritual conferences. They had disclosed to each other their lives, desires and slightest trials. This was to encourage each of them to remain firm under all conditions and they wanted to give some act of suffering to Our Lord. Also, they went voluntarily deep into the forest several times during the week and would tear their shoulders with willow shoots, which Catherine had been doing for a long time by herself and in her particular manner.

They had consecrated themselves entirely to Our Lord with all of the worldly courage they could harness. They were more admirable and esteemed than the others, because they lived in innocence and what they did to repent for their sins was done for the love of God.

Chapter 11

In this manner, from day to day, God had fortified Catherine Tekakwitha and prepared her soul for the great trial she had to pass in the coming summer. It was a trial touching something very sensitive to her, but by the grace of Our Lord she would come out victorious. As it is one of the most beautiful passages in the story of her life, I believe is pleasing to say it here and interrupting this history of her life.

Her adopted sister had acted as the mistress of the cabin and pretended through right of age to have authority over her because she regarded her younger sister in a worldly manner. She tried to persuade her to marry, rather for the use that she could be to her than for Catherine's own good. Catherine was held in such a great esteem throughout the village due to her wisdom and piety that there was not a young man who would not have been content to agree to such a marriage. He would consider himself fortunate to have found such a good wife. If her sister succeeded in her plan, it would be of great benefit to the family, because among the Natives it was the customary to give all of what the husband brought from the hunt to the women of the cabin.

She had foreseen great difficulty with Catherine, who she knew was opposed to marriage. She had ignored the persecutions that this generous girl suffered in her own country from the same thing, and the faithfulness with which she prevailed over them. However, she hoped to win her over on the strength of the reasons that she had prepared, and resolved not to be dissuaded. She would either gain her consent or else force her in the matter.

One day, she had taken Catherine aside with a seemingly affectionate and gentle manner. This the reader will not find difficult to believe and if he knows that the Natives are clever and have a good sense and they are naturally eloquent especially when they have a point to gain. She said to her, "It must be admitted, my dear sister, that you have a great obligation to Our Lord for having brought us here from our miserable country, where you can work for your salvation in peace of mind without anything to trouble your devotion. If you are content to be here, I am no less content to see you here with us. Increase this happiness from your wise conduct; it will come on you the esteem and approval of the entire village. There is just one thing you could do that will make me entirely pleased with you and make yourself perfectly content. This is to think seriously of establishing yourself with a good marriage. This is the course followed here from all the girls, and you are of a marriageable age and need it even as the others to remove you from the occasions of sin and supply you with the necessities of life. It is a pleasure for your brother-in-law and me to provide you, as we have done before now, but you know he is getting old and we have a large family. If anything should happen to us and we could not aid you, from where would you get your aid? Believe me, my dear sister; you should place yourself beyond the possibility of the pains of poverty for the good of your soul and body and have the thought to avoid them while you are able to do so easily for the advantage of yourself and your entire family, who desire it."

Catherine was strangely surprised by this discourse that she did not expect. Catherine was very honest and had a great respect of her sister. She did not show the pain this caused her and she even thanked her of her good advice. She then said, as the affair was of such a great consequence, that she wanted to think it over.

This courageous virgin was not offended, but she eluded the first attempt. Immediately she had sought me to complain gently about her sister concerning the entire affair. Then I had said, "Catherine, you are the judge in this matter. It depends on you alone and think of it well, because it is the concern of a great moment." She had immediately replied without hesitation, "Ah, my Father! I will not marry. I do not like men and have the last aversion to marriage. The thing is not possible." In order to sound out and to try her more, which I had continued with upon the strong reasons that her sister presented to her. She had assured me with great firmness in her reply. She said, "The poverty I am threatened with does not scare me, because so little is needed to give to the necessities of this miserable life and my labour could provide for it and I could always find some rags to cover me." Then she returned to the cabin, but I assured her that she was doing right. Catherine did not tell me everything in this conversion. In her own mind, she had already decided her course. It could be said that she was already perfect in her present condition, but she was not content, because her predominating passion was to search always what was right in our holy religion and anything that would make her more pleasing to God. She said to herself in the depths of her heart: there was something over and above the common life of the Sault.

She had even learned and I do not know how, which there were some persons that performed extraordinary penance. She said to her companion, about the missionaries keeping this hidden from her. She had some knowledge of the Evangelical Counsel and a beautiful example of their practice in the Religious Hospitalers Sisters of Saint Joseph. In 1678, Catherine visited Montreal, where she had seen holy virgins in a hospital and they were waiting on the sick with admirable charity and modesty. After having surely considered all these things, Catherine and her companion agreed never to marry. Catherine had dedicated to Jesus Christ her virginity and the other her perpetual widowhood. They had kept this decision a secret and resolved not to speak of it unless absolutely necessary. However, Catherine had found that she could not assist herself on this occasion, because of the pressing insistence of her sister.

After she had returned to the cabin, her sister pressed her again with these words, "Have you thought over of what I told you lately?" She replied, "I have! And if you want me to have respect for you and love you as my sister, never speak to me like that anymore." This chaste girl wanted to silence her sister and place an end to her pressing insistencies. She had told her that she renounced marriage and asked to be allowed to live as she was. She said that she had enough clothes to last her a long time and would work to feed herself without being a burden to her sister or anyone in the village. Catherine's sister was deeply moved by this answer and replied, "My sister, how did you form such a strange resolution? Have you thought seriously of what you are doing? Have you ever seen or heard say of such a thing among the Iroquois girls? Where did you get this strange idea? And could you not see that you expose yourself to the decision of men and temptations of the demon? How could you expect to accomplish what no girl among us has ever done? And forget these thoughts, my dear sister, do not trust your own strength, but follow the custom of the other girls." To all of this, Catherine replied without emotion. She did not fear men speaking to her in a derisive manner as long as she had done nothing wrong. She had hoped that God would give her the necessary strength and to overcome all the temptations of the demon with she was threatened, because her resolution was already taken and she again begged her not to speak of it any more.

It is true, this woman did not want to speak of it again to Catherine, but she told Anastasia, who had taken the place of a mother for the two of them. She had presented her arguments and to have Anastasia on her side. The affair seemed even stranger, because there was no precedent for it, which had appeared difficult and almost morally impossible for Catherine.

It is certain that several girls of her age had tried to restrain themselves from marriage after her death, but they found it difficult and admitted to not having the strength to overcome temptation. The most they could do was to remain widows even though young and in renouncing a second marriage, so as to at least to have some small part in Catherine's crown.

Anastasia was a wise woman and regarded all these reasons with fear. She thought Catherine had taken this resolution lightly and with too much precipitation, and that she would regret it in the future. Anastasia had done all in her capability to change her decision, but like the others she did not succeed. She pressed her with such an insistently that Catherine had replied to her in a voice more firm than usual that if she thought highly enough of marriage she would enter the life, but Catherine wanted to hear nothing more of the matter and stated that no man would mean anything to her.

They separated and came immediately to me; Anastasia to complain of her daughter and Catherine to complain of her mother. The younger of the two reached me first and told me of the suffering caused by her mother and sister, who had both wanted her to marry and found herself incapable of obeying them. To relieve her of her suffering and settle the matter, I had told her to take three more days to consider the subject. She should pray earnestly during that time and recommend her trouble to Our Lord. Also, I would unite with her in prayer and she should attach closely to whatever God inspired her to do within those three days. I had reminded her of being her own mistress in an affair of this sort and the decision would always rest with her alone. Catherine agreed with this plan, but the Holy Spirit influenced her strongly. In less than a quarter of an hour, she came back to search for me.

I was surprised to see her returning a moment after to tell me and all inflamed that she could not live any longer in a situation of indecision from a choice that she had made a long time before. She said while coming near me, "It is settled! It is not a matter to consider and my part has long before been taken. No, my Father! I can have no other spouse but Jesus Christ. I have considered myself content to live in poverty and misery for His love." I will admit here, in good faith, that I wanted to say nothing to Catherine to determine her in this affair, because among the Natives there were so many things opposed to it. I preferred to let God influence His servant directly. It will be successfully concluded that her inspiration came from Him. It was plain to me from her last words that God spoke from the mouth of Catherine; and again, He had inspired in her a decision so heroic.

I finally had taken her part. I had said to her that I praised her resolution and encouraged her to persevere with the same fervour from when she began. I assured that I would defend her against the others, and the other missionaries or I would never abandon her or let her be in want of anything.

I could provide assurance from these few words, which I had removed the soul of Catherine from a strange purgatory and placed her in a sort of paradise. At that moment, she had truly entered into the joy of the Lord and began to feel in the depths of her soul a peace, rest and contentment so great that her exterior became quite changed. It was seen that this peace never left her until her death, and from that time nothing was able to disturb it. This peace was an evident sign from that the spirit of God had possessed her. She had thanked me warmly and left as the most content person in the world. I was filled with admiration, veneration and of an extraordinary joy for her, because it was so heroic of a design. She had the courage to attempt this heroic act, and seeing the divine goodness prepared in this first Iroquois virgin of Our Lord was such a beautiful model of sanctity on this earth and an influential advocate in heaven.

She had no sooner left me when Anastasia came in to state her complaint, saying that Catherine did not want to marry though she was of a marriageable age. I replied to her coldly, because I was astonished that she wanted to torment Catherine about a matter deserving such praise. Anastasia, who had been a Christian for a long time, did not open her eyes to the beauty and merit of such a saintly resolution. And if she had any faith, she should esteem Catherine even more to feel content and honoured, because God had chosen a young girl from her cabin to raise the banner of virginity among the Natives.

A more sudden change could not be thought and Anastasia seemed to have awakened her from a profound sleep, and she blaming herself of her conduct. She would now take the correct view of Catherine's attitude. Anastasia was very holy and admired, praised, encouraged and looked upon Catherine as if she was already a saint. After this, Anastasia was always ready to support Catherine in the life that she had chosen as the better part. She had done more, because she inspired Catherine's sister from the same sentiments. Then the two of them regarded her with greater respect and with a sort of veneration. They had left her in peace and with an entire liberty to do, as she wanted in the future. Our Lord turned this persecution to glory and to the good of His great servant. This was to make known that He was the only Author of this resolution and was unprecedented among the Native girls.

Chapter 12

Catherine was delivered from all these apprehensions and now was in complete power of doing what she deemed right, and being not troubled from anyone. She had thought only of thanking Our Lord for all the graces that she had received from Him. She had corresponded to these graces with gratefulness and with a reciprocal love.

Her companion, who Catherine did not fail to tell the entire affair, had strengthened and aided Catherine. Mary Theresa was always trying to profit from the sentiments Catherine had told to her and from the example she had constantly before her eyes, which was Catherine. Catherine would often say to herself, "Hey what!" And she would say, "If an innocent girl so conducts herself, what should not a sinner like myself do?" It was the fervour of Catherine lighting the fire of divine love in the heart of Mary Theresa, and was a great aid to Catherine's fervour.

Catherine continued on with all her exercises of piety that we have already spoken of. She fortified them through a fervent reception of the sacraments. They were a source of grace, because of the holy dispositions that she brought to them. She began again, even though she was infirm, to chastise her body from continual work, night vigils, fasting and all the sorts of other austerities that were done in secret with only her companion to witness and to join her in them.

She had passed all summer in this manner. We proposed that she should go to the hunt during the winter, but she would not hear of it and protesting that she would never again do so. As we have already said, she had taken this resolution because of the pain she suffered the winter before when being far from the chapel and the holy sacraments. Also, she would have been deprived of all the spiritual aids that she would have in the village.

I had wanted to take her on the hunt as to restore her health a little, as she would not be deprived of the good nourishment that she needed but could not have in the village. The winter was long, and in staying she would suffer through it, because during the winter they lived only on corn. At these words, she had only laughed at this and a moment later she assumed that devout look when she would come to tell me of her spiritual desires. She had given me this reply and dignified of Tekakwitha, "Ah, my Father! It is true the body fares well in the forest, but the soul would languish there and dies of hunger. Whereas in the village, the body would suffer a little from not being so well nourished, but the soul is near to Our Lord and finds entire satisfaction. I have abandoned this miserable body to hunger and any other misery so my soul could be content and have its usual nourishment." She remained in the village for the entire winter and found what she had so eagerly sought; that is to say, crosses of sustenance and all the sweetness of heaven for her spirit. These she had acquired generously for herself in accordance with her custom. Our Lord promised to satisfy those who would hunger and thirst for justice. He had accorded to her these with an equal abundance.

This spirit has this year, 1678, united all those women who number thirteen and having Catherine among them. They have as their purpose the highest condition of perfection. They would assemble themselves and one makes a brief exhortation or they tell their faults and incite virtue upon one another. They are called the Sisters of Catherine, and act like the Daughters of Mercy in France. They do works of charity for their neighbours, especially in taking care of the poor and the sick. They would carry wood in secret to them during the evening and leave immediately for the fear of being perceived. They would go to watch the sick and bring them alms with other things that they would need. Poverty punishes the mission from time to time and would follow the Natives everywhere.

To have attained their end, they make the practice of mortification and are opposed to carnal pleasures, which they treat as the bait of the demon. They said that the Fathers who want to make them abandon the penitential belt and discipline do not know how much they were burden with sins before they were taught to live rightly. They assist one another in the fields and are always seen as occupied in carrying wood or making wampum collars, planting, spinning, sewing, making pouches and in other labours. After the death of Catherine, one of them from Onondaga, Mary Barbara Attontinon, had pronounced the vows of the Sister at the Congregation of Notre-Dame in Montreal.

As we have said before, the mission was at the time very fervent under the guidance of its missionaries. It was a new Church possessed with extraordinary graces and holiness prevailing there. This was worthy of the early Church.

The Iroquois had become strongly attached to the Church. These ardent and brave converts had conceived with such a grief and shame of the sins from their past lives, although these had been erased through the baptisms and the great penance that they are still performing. Several times a week, some of them chastised their bodies until they bled. Also, while gathering firewood for entire days, they would wear iron belts around their bodies. Joseph Togoniron, who was the famous Chief of the Sault with the name of the Great Macqua, wore an iron belt every Friday and on all the great feasts. Paul Honoguenhag, a Huron, was the first catechist of the mission. He was appointed Chief for the observance of Christianity and religion, and did as much penance. Another Huron catechist called Stephan was of such austere virtue that it gave devotion by merely seeing him pray.

The women were not behind their husbands in the ardour they showed for a life of penance. They always went to extremes and when it came to our knowledge, we were obliged to moderate their zeal. I saw Mary of Onondaga, during three consecutive nights and through the severest weather, rolled in the snow to atone for her past sins. Another had done so in a similar cold and was accompanied by such a heavy snowstorm, where it was not possible to see two steps from oneself or having the strength to stand, but she stood and stripped to the waist while reciting the Rosary in this posture. It should be stated here that in her language, the Hail Mary is twice as long as in our own.

Others went even further. In the middle of winter, having broken the ice with their hatchets, they plunged themselves up to their necks in rivers and ponds. Often they had the courage to recite several decades of the Rosary while enduring this frightful torment. They would come out with a vest of ice around their bodies.

Mary Theresa Tegaiaguenta went down to the river one freezing night while the rest were tired from a long hunt and deep into their sleep. She broke the ice and kept her body immersed in the water while reciting the entire Rosary of the Blessed Mary. When this courageous woman had left the water, she passed the rest of the night on her mat in her frozen clothing. This was a new penance, but having staying in longer would be a harder penance. She did the same the next night and then again the third night. Her weak flesh could not sustain the vigour of her spirit, and she caught a violent fever and nearly died.

Anne equalled in virtue that of her husband, who was the good Christian Stephan. She was not satisfied with plunging herself into the river through the ice so she also had plunged her little daughter Mary, aged three, and pulled her out half dead. When I had blamed her later of this action, I asked her of the reason that led her to do it. She replied simply and in good faith that she had the child do penance in advance for fear of when the child grew older that she would fall into sin.

I had the charge of the greater number of these people, but all of these things were everyday occurrences in the forest, where these fervent Christians believed that everything there was permitted to them. The woman, who had plunged into the icy river on three consecutive nights was not accustomed to going on the hunt and only went this time because

I would not allow her to do as she wanted in the village. She said to herself, "At least I shall be the mistress of my own body in the forest." She had admitted this when they brought her to me more dead than alive. All we could do in these situations was to prevent a repetition of these excesses, but the good intentions and absence of understanding of the new Christians had rendered their actions excusable.

I will admit that these excesses are not always a sure mark of sanctity, because vanity and the admiration for themselves would advance into them. However, we have reason to believe that these Christians are a true sign, because they persevered throughout the rest of their lives. They had lived in great innocence, union and charity, especially in regards to the poor and sick. They did not content themselves in working to their own salvation, but were also zealous for their fellow countrymen coming to the Sault either to visit or live with them. They could be seen instructing them all day and even at night, because these newcomers did not immediately go from one extreme to the other. They brought with them some sort of conduct that at the least disturbance would have thrown the entire village into dismay. And to have prevented this, the men and the women of the Holy Family made the rounds of the cabins. They had voluntarily set apart their sleep to prevent offences to God.

The zeal of these fervent Christians had extended beyond the Great River to Montreal. A great number of people at the time had descended from the Outaouacs to trade in Montreal. The Natives were accustomed to going there and profiting from the general trade. The Great Macqua and Kinnouskouen, who was a Macqua catechist and an elder of the Sault, were more interested in the things of God than their own affairs. They had performed a deed worthy of eternal commemoration. It is well known that these trading times were days of drunkenness and impurity. These two Christians, having the influence among the Natives, assembled the girls and women in a separate place to camp, which they had then guarded all night long to prevent the girls and women from leaving and also to protect from the men entering it.

The same two persons, with the good Stephan, went to preach the Gospel in the village of the Macquas. During the time they had spent there, they preached all day long in the longhouses without taking any rest and received during the night those who came to see them for advice in their difficulties. All of this they did during a time of drunkenness, making our faith triumph. They had preached quite openly without the fear of being killed by the drunken people. Their zeal was not in vain, because God blessed their work and they secured great fruits to our religion.

Martin Skandegonrhaksen, a very near relative of the Great Macqua, went to preach the faith in the country of the Macquas with the others. He would preach the Gospel openly in the village among the elders. The spirit of the prayer gave him a habit of wearing his Rosary around his head. The Great Macqua profited from his dying words throughout the remainder of his life. Martin died in 1675, at the age of twenty years old, two years after his baptism.

If the European nations would stop with their cursed liquor trade and licentiousness that ruined the missionaries' work, and the free use of firearms in the war that followed, we would have fine churches in this country. However, thanks be to God that for many years we still had among the Natives a large number who had preserved in innocence and fervour.

However, since virtue is produced through herself, it was that several people doubted themselves in the village. Catherine would be among them and she had an eager and penetrating spirit. She thought there was something above this piety of the Sault, something hidden in these Christians that was the source or the support of their virtue. Finally, she had reached such a high degree of virtue that she discovered part of it and concluded the rest. To satisfy her, I was obliged to give her a discipline and a little belt of iron, which she had employed from that time forth and to place an end to her extreme thirst of suffering. If I had left her to herself in this matter, she would have soon have surpassed the others. She would chastise herself unmercifully, but her strength was not nearly equal to her courage. It was necessary to moderate her courage so as though not to exhaust her strength. Even though of all the precautions I had taken, she was able to evade me at times. This happened during the same winter on the feast of the Purification, Thursday February 2, 1679. She had imitated the holy ceremonies of the Church, on which processions were customary to that day. She gave Our Lady proof of the love she endured for Her. Catherine had walked around her long field while she recited the Rosary several times, all the while being buried up to her waist in the snow.

Something quite important had happened to her lately, which Father Chauchetiere and I could not marvel enough at while having scourged herself as usual with admirable ardour and in a very dark place. She found herself surrounded with such a great light and as if it were high noon. Although it had lasted as the first shower of her stripes that is, to speak of her scourging, because she had scourged herself many times. I could judge from what she had told me, which this light had lasted two or three repeated good Miserere; that is to say,

Psalm fifty-one. We have no cause to believe that there is any illusion in all this, because she is quite foreign to deceit and is very humble.

We have every reason to believe that it is a grace granted from Our Lord to His faithful servant, who is entirely His. She had served Him with innocence and fervour, and was capable of ravishing the angels.

In her great and glorious title of virgin, Catherine was more blessed than the others. She attained a higher place among the Natives of the Sault and all of those who had embraced the faith in Northern France. She was the first in the New World from a particular inspiration of the Holy Spirit had consecrated her virginity to Jesus Christ. Catherine, from a pure choice and ardent desire to please God, had embraced this condition so perfect and so sublime.

Chapter 13

The Fathers of the Church disputed with competitive spirit to know which virtues of Our Lady had rendered Her most pleasing in the eyes of God and worthy of being His Mother. There are some who had thought the reason was Her virginity. They thought from being the greatest among all pure creatures, by an intentional vow, that she had raised the divine standard of virginity throughout the world. Our Lady had surpassed all the grace, perfection and sanctity of all the other saints together. I say the same to proportion of an act so heroic that it was done by this young virgin in following the example of the Queen of Virgins.

Catherine had a quick and observant mind. She would study every means to testify more and more of her love for Jesus Christ. She was devoted to examining everything that was done to please the Lord and would immediately place what she had learned into practice. This was the reason that while having passed some days at Montreal in 1679, she for the first time had seen Sisters and was so charmed with their modesty and devotion. She had informed herself most thoroughly with regard to the manner that these holy Sisters were living and the virtues they were practicing. She learnt they were Christian virgins consecrated to God through a vow of perpetual chastity.

She would give me no peace until I granted her permission to make the same sacrifice of herself. It was her greatest glory before God, and considering her from that aspect alone, it is not astonishing that she deserved to receive so many graces during her lifetime, and to bring about such great miracles after her death. She served God, Him alone, and her only desire was to please Him. God had preserved her, because she was for more than twenty years in an angelic purity of soul and body. She had aided herself in this preparation of renouncing marriage from a resolution to guard her virginity, which was contrary to the custom of the other girls. He prepared her through generously raising her above the persecutions that she had suffered because she did not want to marry. Almost as soon as she arrived at the Sault, Catherine had resolved to lead a life of virginity and had kept this a secret until again being persecuted, which obliged to disclose her decision.

After Catherine had declared that she would prefer to accomplish her purpose without any further delay. She wanted as soon as possible to belong only to Jesus Christ, to sacrifice herself and make a promise that could not possibly be repealed. The thing was so unusual and appeared differently with the life of the Natives. I had thought it right not to rush the matters and give her plenty of time to consider carefully a matter of such consequence. I tried her, therefore, again for some time. Following this, I saw the great progress that she had made in every sort of virtue, and above all with what profusion God would communicate with His servant.

I was again convinced that it was the spirit of God that was acting in this excellent girl; that is to say, it seemed to me the purpose of Catherine could come from no other source than from Him. Forthwith, I gave at last the permission she desired. It would be difficult to place in words of the joy she felt and the fervour with which she had prepared for such great an act. When this day came, so long for, that it was the happiest and most beautiful day of her life. She made one last effort to offer her sacrifice to Jesus with all the piety, all the devotion and all the ardour she was capable of.

It was the feast of the Annunciation, Saturday March 25, 1679, at eight o'clock in the morning. A moment after Jesus Christ gave Himself to her in Holy Communion, Catherine Tekakwitha completely gave herself to Him. She renounced marriage forever with a vow of perpetual virginity for Him and in imitation of the holy Sisters. With a heart all embraced with His love, she begged Him to be her only Spouse and accept her as His bride. She prayed to the Mother of God, as she had a tender devotion and to present herself to Her divine Son. Then she wanted to make a double consecration in one single act at the same time she devoted herself to Jesus Christ. She consecrated her entire self to Mary and asking Her instantly to be very well her Mother and take her as Her daughter.

After she passed some hours at the foot of the altar, she was always on her knees in holy meditation and in perfect union with God. In this manner, a great act had taken place and the greatest desire of Catherine was achieved. I had surely thought that such a resolution must have been inspired in her through the Holy Spirit. I have found it difficult to describe the devotion of a soul, which the spouse of Jesus Christ was already so full of pious unction and offered her sacrifice to God. The angels, who stood looking on as witnesses, knew and were surely in admiration of this thing difficult to do. It was from an eminent of a soul and the burning love in a woman. They were overwhelmed with joy when they beheld this Native girl placed with them through a vow of chastity. In truth, after her heroic sacrifice had been made, she no longer seemed of this world and led a life most like to those of the angels. Her conversation was to heaven and her soul had already tasted of its gentleness while she mortified her body through her new austerities. It was related to her intense striving so deep in her mind to be constantly united to God.

She eventually exhausted her strengths and she had fell more ill in the same summer and scarcely escaped death. She retained a great pain in her stomach that was accompanied with frequent vomiting with a low fever that was gradually undermining her. This brought her to a condition of weakness from which she was not able to raise herself. Regardless of her infirmities, it took courage such as hers to support these sufferings. All the fervour of her devotions never lessened until she died. On the contrary, her spirit seemed to have taken new strength at the expense of her body and she sought new means to sanctify herself as she approached the end of her days.

The just persons are admirable in their own manners and the more they had realized their end is near, the more rapidly they would advance in perfection. They are holy misers and never content with what they have given to God, but they always wanted to give Him more and receive more from

Him in return. This was to have gathered greater riches to their eternity.

This chaste girl had accumulated a large number of riches for her eternity during the two years and a half that she lived at the Sault. This was from the remarkable things she accomplished there and we have seen here, and even more from the constant practice of Christian virtues. She possessed such an eminent degree of things that it would be difficult to judge the one that shone forth the most. The nearer she approached the end of her days, the more visibly she shone forth in all these virtues because she practiced all these virtues with such edification. Although I have already given some beautiful examples of her virtues, and before speaking of her death, I want to say a bit more concerning the one that is the most admirable in the saints and is the only virtue leading to real sanctity.

Chapter 14

Charity is not only the queen of the virtues, but it gives value to all the other virtues and is the source of sanctity. Charity is the shortest and most assured road for arriving at sanctity. To be soon a saint and perfect there is need only to love God with one's entire heart to attain that end. Although one would appear holy and perfect before man, without this virtue one is nothing before God, according to Saint Paul. With this in my mind, it is not difficult to believe that Catherine had become perfect in such a short time considering the ardour of charity she had for God. She loved Him so much that her joy was to think and continually offer Him all her thoughts, words and actions.

She had particularly liked to be alone and made friends with the two women we have mentioned above merely because that they led her to God. If one would happily hear of a conversion about something one loves, Catherine would find an extraordinary happiness in hearing about God. She received such pleasure from this. It was sufficient only to begin a pious discourse in her presence, which would make have her leave whatever she was doing. Immediately, she would collect her thoughts and listen to the discourse with all the attention without ever tiring.

In 1680, the last year of her life, she had to stay almost continually in her cabin due to her illness. Father Chauchetiere took care of her. He would see her everyday and conversed with her of God and continued explaining to her our mysteries. For his gratefulness, she gave this Father many graces after her death. She had even appeared to him several times. She had prophesied things to him and guided him interiorly in the highest perfection with as much grace.

Her love of God did not end at simple affection, as she always sought every possible means to give Him proof of it. It was sufficient for her to hear of some mortification of the saints, which she would immediately imitate without giving importance to how hard it was to endure. She had mortified herself using fire, wearing iron belts and through other means that we shall see a little later when we speak of her austerities and her love of the cross.

The most authentic evidence of her ardent love for God was pressed from a strong desire to please Him, because her God was Jesus Christ who she had consecrated her virginity to. She renounced marriage to have Jesus Christ as her Spouse. This was unheard among her people and all the more to be admired in Catherine, because those of her gender were supported by what a husband brings home from the hunt. Also, they have a desire for marriage and consider the greatest happiness possible in this life when they have met a good hunter.

CATHERINE TEKAKWITHA: BOOK TWO

God had never allowed His creatures to surpass Him in love and gave Himself to her with such profusion that it was necessary to see this as to believe it. It has been told of by several saints that at times their hearts were so inflamed with the divine love, that in spite of the efforts they took to hide this sacred fire, which consumed them from within, they were not able to prevent the escape of some of its sparks. Such was Catherine's love.

This young Native girl was so filled with the spirit of God and had tasted the gentleness in its possession. Her entire exterior was a testimony of this spirit of God and her eyes, gestures and words were filled with divine love at such moments. If one were with her it did not take long to be touched by this divine love and become warmed with this heavenly fire. This charity that Catherine had for God was the source of her great love to the Holy Eucharist and the cross. These are the two means by which the Saviour of the world proved His love for us the most. Men owe Him that reciprocity, which Catherine had given in a marvellous manner.

It would be difficult to bring further the faith, the esteem and the tenderness that she had felt for the Holy Eucharist. From the time, she had the knowledge of this great sacrament, she remained devoted to and delighted by the Holy Eucharist until her death. We have seen her assiduity in doing her duty to God, the long prayers at the chapel, the fervour in her communions, the many tears that she had poured forth for her love at the foot of the altar and the entire days spend there, even during the coldest weather in New France.

She so often forgotten the wants of her body, and her entire body was benumbed from the cold. Often having seen her entire body frozen, I was inspired to make her leave the chapel and enjoy the warmth of the fire with us. Then a moment later, she would escape me and say with a little smile that she was not cold. This was done to return to the place where she had left her heart. The fire of her love had triumph over the bite of the cold. What have the French to say regarding this, because they would pass our chapels a hundred times a day without entering even once to greet Our Lord on His altar. They are so bored in the chapel because the mass they are obliged to hear is a little long.

Catherine had a great love for her beloved Jesus in the Holy Eucharist and would have a devotion to Our Saviour on the cross. These two mysteries, the Holy Eucharist and the Passion of Our Lord had ceaselessly occupied her spirit and burned in her heart the purest flames of love. Everyday she was seen to pass entire hours at the foot of the altar, and she would not move and as if transported beyond her physical body. Also, to ensure this thought in her mind she always wore around her neck a small copper crucifix that I had given her and she would frequently kiss it with feelings of gratefulness. She would kiss her crucifix every day and night with great sentiments of the recognition of her love for Jesus Christ, for she had so shown the kindness of our redemption and the tender compassion to the sufferings of Jesus. She not only had the cross hanging from her neck, she also carried her cross in her body that was after Him, the divine Master, and together with all the saints.

He had guided Catherine throughout her entire life and inspired her with a holy hatred of herself. It was so much recommended from Jesus Christ and necessary for salvation. She even went further and wanted to share His pains. After having consecrated her heart to Our Lord in the Blessed Sacrament, she sacrificed her body to the cross and was never separated from the cross.

She had treated her body with such harsh punishment, and she was skilful in inventing other means of afflicting and crucifying her flesh at the Sault. This she did through labour, loss of sleep, fasting, cold, fire, irons and pointed belts that she often wore all day during the summer heat, the winter cold and with hunger. She punished her body with a thousand or twelve hundred stripes bloody stripes over her shoulders several times a week. It would be difficult anywhere else to find such innocence, and it was joined with such austere penance. She had a great desire for mortification.

In the winter, she went to the forest with her sister and the other women. She had always remained behind to remove her moccasins and walked barefoot in the snow and over the ice. She would be careful to put her moccasins on again before she could be seen, because she was very humble that she had preferred not to be seen mortifying herself.

Once Catherine had asked Anastasia which was the severest penance that she considered to be the most pleasing sacrifice and to prove the love to Our Lord. The other answered, "My daughter, I know of nothing on earth more terrible than fire." Catherine replied, "I myself, no more." Catherine said no more about it then. In the evening when everyone went to sleep, she spent a long time burning her legs with an iron in the same manner that slaves are burned among the Iroquois. In this manner, she had declared herself the slave of her Saviour. She then presented herself at the door of the chapel in the darkness of the night and enduring her beautiful marks of the cross to have offered what she had suffered for her dear Spouse in the Holy Sacrament of the altar.

Another time, she and her companion decided when they were alone to place a burning coal between their toes because it was supposed to be the most sensitive to the pain of fire. After Catherine admitted to her companion having done it and keeping the burning coal between her toes for a long time, Mary Theresa was astonished because she did not think Catherine could have done so without some sort of miracle.

On Monday March 25, 1680, she made a last effort of love and gratefulness to Jesus immolated on our altars and on the cross. It was prompted by an intense desire to give all things to Him that day after preparing herself with new devotions, during Holy Communion, she made a perpetual offering of her soul to Jesus in the Holy Eucharist and her body to Jesus crucified. She took Him again as her only Spouse and devoted herself completely to Him as His bride. She had chosen again the great feast of Our Lady, to make her offering to the Son of God through the hands of His divine Mother and to take her once more for Her own. I could say after she renewed her vow, her soul had lived only for Jesus in the Holy Eucharist, and her body lived only as to die with Him on the cross that is in the midst of sorrow and suffering. I would say die on the cross, because she had truly died on the cross and shortened her days from an act worthy of eternal remembrance. About two or three months before her death, this generous girl had desired to attach herself even more to the cross of her Saviour. Because of her continual infirmities, she was to testify through some heroic act of the strong passion that she had to participate in His sufferings. As if she had done nothing before then, she decided in imitation of Saint Benedict and Blessed Aloysius Gonzaga, whom I had spoken of to her.

She gathered a large bundle of thorny branches with big sharp thorns and hid them in her cabin. When everyone was asleep, she scattered these thorny branches upon her mat and then slept on them and having only her blanket over her body. She had the strength not only to roll herself all night long upon these thorns that pierced so deeply into her flesh, but also to do this for the following three nights. The pain was unimaginable. She confessed to me her pain after she had done this. This act had left her so haggard and exhausted that her face resembled that of a dead person. As having not known the real cause of this, we attributed the change in her to her ordinary infirmities, which had appeared to us as increasing visibly everyday without knowing the true cause. Her companion suspected that she was hiding something and then she succeeded in having Catherine confessed the truth to her. Catherine further said of the thought to continue doing this until her death. Her companion replied, "Yes, but do you know well it is offending God by doing this sort of excess without having the permission of your confessor?" The shadow of the sin made Catherine discover this beautiful action, which without this only apprehension that she would have kept this hidden for all her life.

She sought me immediately. She approached me with these words, "Ah, my Father! I have sinned." Then she had told me of the entire affair and in my heart I admired her, but I was angry and blamed her for not being prudent. I had ordered her to throw these thorns into the fire to prevent her from renewing it, and she did it with great submission. She had possessed this virtue to an eminent degree and was always ready to do or leave undone, and was equally content to be on either side without being attached to her own will. This was an infallible proof of the spirit of God influencing her. It was with reason that the fear of sin made Catherine confess an action so much to her merit. In truth, she had an extreme horror for sin and even the shadow of the sin, above all having a surprising scrupulous of a conscience. This was particularly evident in her confessions, where she always accompanied then with sobs and tears. She did her confessions with a complete discussion of her smallest faults.

She considered herself the greatest sinner of the village and had such a humble opinion of herself. She could not endure anyone to say the smallest word of her praise. If someone would praise her, she would immediately leave or if she were not able to leave, she would cover herself in her blanket to hide her blushing face. It even afflicted her when I said to her, "Great glory is waiting for you in paradise!" Her sudden reply was that she could by no means understand through what right or title such a miserable creature, as she believed herself to be, and someone so guilty of so many sins, was to promise herself the reward prepared to the saints. She had regarded herself as worthless, but she thought highly of everyone else by praising and approving those who merited it and excusing the rest with great charity. The Natives were very much disposed to malicious talk about others, but never a word against anyone ever came from her mouth.

Catherine was from a nature that was gentle, honest, affectionate, kind and even joyful in spirit and was always ready to aid someone. Her patience while in the midst of her continual suffering had appeared heroic to us. She endured her sufferings with a constant and evenness of spirit that delighted us. She was always joyful and contented without ever manifesting impatience or showing the least sign of annoyance and sadness, except for the time that her sister pressed her with insistency to marry.

CATHERINE TEKAKWITHA: BOOK TWO

The last two months of her life that she had endured extraordinary sufferings. She was obliged to hold herself in the same position the entire day and night. When she would move, she did so with extreme pain. She never once in that time ever given sighs in complaint, but she esteemed herself most content when these pains were at their worst. She spoke of wanting to live and die on the cross by uniting her sufferings to those of her Saviour.

She had a high idea of the faith and all it teaches, and a particular respect for those called from God to make the faith known throughout the world. Her modesty was charming and her entire exterior a certain air of virtue and of piety that inspired others. Her courage was heroic. Her faithfulness to the service of God was inviolable. Her tears as well as her union with God were constant. Her devotion was tender and even to the point of tears. Her communion with God was intimate and uninterrupted and she never lost sight of Him. It was this that raised her in so short a time to such a sublime manner of compassion. Then she was raised in such short a time and a sublime condition of piety. Catherine had an evangelical purity and she was so zealous and persevered even to her last breath. She possessed a remarkable gift of prayer without having had any other teacher than the Holy Spirit. In a few words, she had possessed all the virtues eminently and this could be seen throughout the course of her life.

The virtue that seemed proper of Catherine and the virtue that raised her merit the most was purity. In its evident meaning, it signified an exemption from sin. The other more usual signification is understood as an entire freedom from the vice of impurity. In regards to the first, I do not think she ever offended God by committing a mortal sin. I would say more that she had such a real horror for sin that it kept her in such a great vigilance to preserve herself from it. I do not know if in the two years and a half that she lived at the Sault that she ever committed any grievances and even the smallest or deliberate fault. She always took such particular care to avoid even the slightest faults.

This is what is said as being truly holy and possessing perfect charity. What concerns the other or second purity, I say and shall always say, was a miracle of grace. I cannot understand that how Catherine passed her life in her country and at the Sault and remained virgin in body and soul without ever during all that time feeling the least thing contrary to this virtue either in body or soul. This I would say appears unbelievable, but it is true. She already told me of her own accord, but wanting to be assured still more concerning such marvellous a thing, I asked her after I had given her the Holy Viaticum on the evening before her death. Even though she had difficulty speaking, she made an effort to reply to me in a firm tone of voice, "No! No!" With a gesture testifying the pain she felt in still being asked at her death concerning a sin that she so strongly held in horror during her life. It was this love of purity what caused her heart to be so tender an affectionate for the Queen of Virgins.

God chose this one of her race to be the first Iroquois virgin to have consecrated her virginity to Our Lord. God had protected her with His blessings from the womb of her mother. From this source came her tender affection for Our Lady, the Queen of Virgins and the Mother of Purity. As soon as Catherine learned about Her, she had loved Her ecstatically and spoke of Her with enthusiasm. She had learned from her heart the litanies composed in Her honour and said them every evening in privacy following the common prayers of the cabin. She never went without her Rosary. She would recite it in all her goings and comings. She had signalized Saturdays and the other days dedicated to the Mother of Mercy with some mortification or by some act of extraordinary virtue. Catherine had prepared herself with increased fervour when came Her most solemn feast days. Those great days were to her a time of spiritual renewal. She had taken much pleasure in these feast days and she would receive so many graces. We have seen that on these feast days, she would offer some great sacrifice to Our Lord. This was like her vow of virginity that she made partly to imitate the Holy Virgin, because to give Her this eminent proof of her esteem and love.

Finally, from when she had taken the resolution at the Sault to have Jesus Christ as her Spouse, she also took Mary as her Mother. She had thrown herself into Her arms, abandoning herself entirely to Her guidance with all filial confidence of a daughter worthy of such a Mother. Catherine, we believe, obtained from a reciprocal love such a marvellous and rare gift of purity from Her divine Son.

Catherine would have wanted with Saint Paul, which everyone would have done as her. The manner of her actions, reputation and a certain indefinable something was seen by the French and the Natives in this young virgin. She was the most fervent of the entire village and would go on to do some amazing things. She has done the marvel of our forests. She had caused several people of wanting to learn from her lips what was most agreeable to God, so they could go forth and do it. If she tried to hide herself that she could not refuse instructing others.

Virginity, chastity and continence were the subjects of Catherine's discourses. She had spread them as a balm everywhere. She spoke of these virtues so that they might be embraced or to detest vice. Although she had never mentioned anyone of these subjects without giving some praise of the Mother of God. It could be judged at these times that her tongue spoke from the depths of her heart, because it was filled with admiration, veneration and tenderness for her incomparable Mother who was her refuge in everything and she attempted earnestly to imitate Her. The manner Catherine spoke of Her, we allowed ourselves to think that she had seen the Mother of God.

Chapter 15

After telling the life and virtues of this Iroquois virgin at length, I have now come to her death. If Catherine Tekakwitha died where she was born, I would take the words of the Sage. I would say of her what he had said of the just man; that is to say, she was taken from this world in the springtime of her life from a very particular act of providence from God. In time, this innocent soul would become contaminated by the corruption of her country, where He hastened to remove her from the iniquities surrounding her. Although Catherine had ended her life gloriously in very fervent mission, it was because of this that I would prefer to take the other thought of the Sage. This is to say that Catherine left this earth only because she was ready to be in heaven. She achieved her purpose, being content enough to accomplish in only four years what others had difficulty bringing about after many years and reaching a great age.

Catherine was small and walked with a limp because of an injury to her foot she received when she was nineteen years old. She was very infirm and nearly always ill. About a year before her death, a great illness left her with a slow fever and severe pain in her stomach. This was accompanied with frequent vomiting caused, without any doubt, by her continual work, night vigils, fasting and other excessive austerities, and especially from her poor eyesight. She continued these excessive austerities without ever ceasing until her death, and as a final proof, I remember the agonizing mat of thorns that this generous girl lessened her remaining health. The fever made it all the worse, as it finally obliged her to stay on her mat. At the end of two months, it took her from us. Her last days were truly precious days of grace and holiness for Catherine. She passed them in the exercise of all those excellent virtues, which she had so practiced during her lifetime and never shone so brilliantly as at her death. At the time of her death, we saw her faith, hope, charity, humility, gentleness, patience, resignation and her surprising happiness in the midst of her suffering.

Father Chauchetiere had charge of the sick. He visited Catherine everyday in her cabin during her last illness and the Father could not admire her enough. He had always found her with a smiling face. This clearly showed the peace of her soul and the pleasure that she had found in her pains. We must not be astonished of this holy girl. She lived on the cross with her Saviour and Spouse, and she had the joy to follow His example by dying on the cross.

While all the men were at the hunt and the women, who remained in the village, were occupied from morning until night in the forest or the fields, they would leave their sick alone all day with a plate of sagamite and a little water within their reach. In this abandoned condition, that Catherine passed her time during her last illness. What was ordinary a cause of pain and annoyance for the sick was for her an occasion of new merit and even of new consolation. She had known to profit from all things, because she had accustomed herself for a long time to commune with God. She had employed of this solitude to attach herself more to Him and to become more inflamed with His love.

In her innermost soul, she was delighted in her God with an abundance of joy and spiritual satisfaction that were the most pure, because she was detached from worldly affairs. To bring these to the source of her delight, she went to the chapel every day until she was not able to move. She did this because her centre of affection was the Holy Eucharist. She would adore Him and pass entire hours in gentle company with Him, which held such a charm for her, even though her great weakness made it difficult. When it was not capable to do this, she had made her Stations of the Cross of the Passion of Christ there in spirit, and uniting herself to the perpetual sacrifice of our altars with a continual sacrifice for her entire self to Our Saviour.

It would take too long to explain the extent of her patience, humility, obedience, simplicity, faithfulness, her union with God, the greatness of her devotion to the Blessed Virgin and to her Guardian Angel. She excelled so greatly in all virtues and she gave us such rare examples of these virtues. It seems as if each one had been her particular virtue. It has happened that so holy of a life was crowned with an exceptional death. It is repeated of Catherine, as in the short time that she fulfilled, she accomplished what was needed for a long time; that is, she was already ripe for heaven. What she did in the four years after baptism, others have difficulty achieving during a very long life. Catherine had ended her life in the flower of her youth, because she was only twenty-four years old when she left it.

When the time of her last moments had approached, her strength was becoming weaker until the beginning of Holy Week, being Palm Sunday. God wanted to take her from this world so that she could go, as we have every reason to believe, to celebrate the following feast days with the angels.

On Tuesday morning, seeing that she was approaching death, we gave her the Holy Viaticum or the last Holy Communion. All of the Natives at the village had accompanied the Blessed Sacrament to Catherine's cabin. They were charmed by such edifying piety. She had received the sacrament with an angelic love and devotion, as a true spouse of Jesus Christ.

Those recent converts were in her cabin could not hold back their tears, because they were the witnesses to a great virtue. I had wanted at the same time to give her the Sacrament of Extreme Unction, which is the anointing of the sick when they are at the verge of death, but she had told me there was then no pressing necessity. From what she said, I thought to defer it to Wednesday morning. The divine Saviour was no sooner with her that she renewed all the offerings. She made to Him deep sentiments of gratefulness for the great graces received from Him, especially at the mission. Catherine had passed the remainder of the day and the following night in communing fervently with Our Saviour, Our Lady and her crucifix. She had repeated the acts that she was so accustomed to in her days of health.

CATHERINE TEKAKWITHA: BOOK TWO

On Wednesday morning, she received Extreme Unction with the same devotion, as for when she had received the Holy Viaticum on the preceding day. At three o'clock in the afternoon, the bell was rung to gather the Natives, who had desired passionately to witness the death of this great servant of God. Three hours after noon, Catherine entered into an agony that was the most gentle in the world.

A short half-hour after her agony, she had pronounced the Holy Names, "Jesus! Mary!" Then a slight spasm had come about at the side of her mouth and she entirely lost the vigour of speech, but her hearing was still very good and she was fully conscience until her last breath. It was evident that she had tried to make with her heart at least those acts when I suggested to her during these last moments. She died peacefully and as if she had entered into a light sleep. This blessed soul had left her virgin body to go with her beloved Spouse. Catherine Tekakwitha died in the twenty-fourth year of her life on Wednesday of Holy Week at three o'clock in the afternoon. She was to celebrate in heaven with Him the triumphs of the cross. She had so much loved and attached her heart, affections, and chaste and virgin body through this life of mortification. Then her face suddenly changed. It appeared so smiling and devout and everyone was extremely astonished. We were all admiring her face, and we could not have tired ourselves looking at her.

The day Catherine had died, we passed with an extraordinary devotion. Immediately, she left the entire village with a fragrance of her virtue and esteem for sanctity, especially a few hours later when I eulogized her at the evening prayers. I made the Natives know of the treasure that they possessed and had lost before they came to know her.

Diego Paoletti

Father Chauchetiere and I remarked the two loves of Catherine. They were Our Lord hidden in the Holy Eucharist and Our Lord Jesus nailed to the cross. And through a particular providence from God, she gave her precious soul to her heavenly Spouse on the Wednesday of Holy Week. Although it was a little before the days when the Institution of the Bread of Life and the Death of the Saviour are celebrated.

Her virgin body was buried the following day at three o'clock in the afternoon. She was buried in the midst of tears from all, who wept not as much from sorrow, but with a public joy that was inspired in the entire village by her holy life. Their hope was that they would have a powerful patroness in heaven. We had made her funeral with great sentiments of veneration, esteem, joy and piety. A joy increased from having Catherine as an influential intercessor near God and from her precious remains that they have always venerated.

She is the support, bulwark and the guiding spirit of this mission. These were the sentiments pronounced from Father Fremin when he heard of the death of Catherine on his return from France, where he went this year concerning the affairs of the Sault. Catherine Tekakwitha had died as she lived; that is to say, as a saint. It was to be expected that such a holy life would be followed with a most holy death, because she was filled with the Holy Spirit.

Chapter 16

The death of Catherine Tekakwitha was accompanied by some interesting circumstances. I believed they were similar to those of the saints, because these circumstances made us judge that the life of Catherine was pleasing to God.

We shall take as the first circumstance what occurred on the day of her death. It seemed that God wanted to reward her for her devotion, because she loved and glorified Him the most. He allured her to Him on Wednesday of Holy Week, the vigil of the two days consecrated to the two great mysteries of the Holy Eucharist and the cross, who were her entire joy and delight. I remember when more than two months before her death, at the beginning of her last illness, Father Chauchetiere had an assertion. The Father asserted that on Holy Wednesday, God would take her from this world. She was to celebrate in heaven the two great feast days of Good

Friday and Easter Sunday, because they were her principal devotions on earth.

The second circumstance is to be as much as admired as the first. It is a praiseworthy custom here for two members of the Holy Family to take turns in watching during the night whenever the sick are in danger of dying. It was asked as to whom should do this for Catherine.

On Tuesday night, the last night of her life, I had named two of the most fervent members, who were Mary of Onondaga and Margaret Gagouithon. Margaret was younger than the other and the youngest of the Holy Family, she was no more than twenty-two years old. Margaret had sought me after the evening prayers for my permission to go in the forest and do some penance. This was to obtain a happy death for Catherine whom she was going to watch because she had loved Catherine, who had also loved her. Catherine saw from some interior vision what this woman did in the darkness of the lonely forest. Margaret followed Catherine for some time before her death. This charity was surprising in a Native girl, because she passed a full quarter of an hour performing penance until she bled on behalf of Catherine. It is still more surprising that the very instant Catherine learned about it while dying on her mat, she turned on her side and asked Mary who was the only one with her that night to have Margaret come immediately.

Mary had obeyed and found Margaret on the way from the forest to her own cabin, where she was going to tighten her means of mortification. She told Margaret, "Catherine is asking for you, so I came to search for you." Then they had entered Catherine's cabin. Catherine asked the young Margaret, who had shown such charity for her, to come closer. Catherine whispered into Margaret's ear, because she wanted to speak to Margaret and have the other rest. In truth, Mary had already fallen asleep. Catherine took hold of Margaret's arm whispered to her, "Approach here, my sister, that I say a little word." Catherine could scarcely talk. Then Catherine held her arm tightly, she said, "Courage, my dear sister, continue with the same fervour you have already began so good." Margaret had no less humility than fervour and replied to Catherine of not knowing her well, because she was a miserable sinner.

Catherine had again took her arm tightly and said, "My sister, I know what I am saying, I also know where you come from and I assure you what you are doing is well done and agreeable to Jesus Christ. Have a good courage, persevere constantly and pray for me at my death, so I could soon leave purgatory. I shall aid you when I am in paradise, be assured." Catherine encouraged and exhorted her to persevere in the service of God and assured her that she was very pleasing to Our Lord, and she promised she would pray for her in heaven. This woman had come to tell me on the following day with a new veneration for Catherine and with a new courage to follow her example, which she is still doing at the mission. When Mary of Onondaga later heard of Catherine's words, she was so consoled by Catherine. She was also encouraged by her words to live always in the same fervour.

A third circumstance related to knowledge concerning the day and even the hour of her death and it could only have come from heaven. After I had given her the Holy Viaticum on Tuesday morning, I wanted to hastily give her Extreme Unction. She told us that there was no haste, because the time had not come. At her words, we deferred the giving of the sacrament until Wednesday morning. We had reason to believe that she would die before noon on that day, but she knew that this was not so.

Catherine's beloved companion and some other women of the Holy Family, who had for about a year formed a small devotional band with Catherine (and is still called the Sisters of Catherine), had greatly desired to be present when she died. They were obliged to go in search of wood for the following feast days, but they were not sure whether to go or to remain with Catherine. They thought the right answer was to ask Catherine. Soon after, I spoke to Catherine for them. She had enough influence in heaven to have her death deferred on their behalf. Catherine said, "Let them go to the forest, they will see me die when they return." At her words, they went and she did not fail them. She remained in the same condition until three o'clock in the afternoon.

After they returned, she waited until everyone entered the cabin. When the last one arrived, she went into her agony and while everyone knelt around her. I saw this marvel with my own eyes. As they had desired, they had the consolation of witnessing the death that she had promised them.

It was said that some time before her last illness, Catherine was digging a grave in the cemetery together with some other women to bury one of her small nephews. The conversation turned to this burial ground, where each of them should have a place. They laughingly asked Catherine where her place was. She said and pointing her finger to a certain place, "There it is!" After her death, Father Chauchetiere did all he could to persuade me to have her placed in the chapel, but to avoid such an unusual thing that I had her grave made in the cemetery. It was the exact place that she had designated. I did not know of her prediction until two years after her burial.

CATHERINE TEKAKWITHA: BOOK TWO

The fourth circumstance is a marvel that I was a witness together with Father Chauchetiere and the Natives. Smallpox had left her face scarred from the age of four. Her infirmities and mortification had contributed to ruin her body even more. Catherine's face was so scarred from smallpox and also before her death she took a very darken complexion. Then her face suddenly transfigured at about a quarter of an hour after her death and became in a moment so beautiful, smiling and white. Her face assumed an appearance of a rosy colour, which she never had, and her features did not appear the same. I immediately saw her face transfigured because I was praying beside her. I cried out, because my astonishment was so great.

I had them go get Father Chauchetiere, who was working at the chapel for the morning of Holy Thursday. He came running with all the Natives upon hearing of this wonder, and we were able to contemplate her face until her burial. This beauty of her face had inspired the love of virtue and everyone was left with their hearts penetrated from the desire of her being a saint. The Natives, who were present, could not restrain the expression of their astonishment. I will admit openly of the first thought that came to me, which was that Catherine might have entered into heaven at that moment. Then, reflecting back in her chaste body, a small ray of the glory she had come to possess.

Two French settlers of La Prairie de la Madeleine had come to the Sault on Thursday morning to assist at the morning mass. They had gone in Catherine's cabin and saw her placed upon her mat with such a beautiful and shining countenance. One of them said to the other, "There is a young woman that sleeps peacefully." He then learning a moment later that she was Catherine. They returned to her cabin and immediately knelt at her feet to recommend themselves to her prayers. This was to satisfy their devotion. They wanted to give public evidence of the veneration that they had for her. At once, they built a coffin for the burial of such a precious relic because they had honoured her as a saint.

The last circumstance of her death is the remarkable effect that she had on the mission. There were piety and fervour at the Sault. It could not be denied after all we have already said. Catherine acquired the remarkable effect of the mission from the beautiful examples of virtue that she had before her eyes, but if at the beginning the mission was a great aid in her sanctification, which approaching the end of her life and particularly at her death, she had served reciprocally in sanctifying the mission.

There was without a delay in seeing this effect on the following day, Good Friday. On Good Friday, all their hearts were so touched at the sight of the cross that Catherine had so loved and kissed. Then I uncovered the cross for them after the sermon on the Passion of Our Lord. I think that there was never seen such a piteous and touching spectacle of devotedness, because everyone began to burst at once with such loud cries and sobs; so much so that it was necessary to let them weep for quite a long time. I had wanted then to intone the Vexilla Regis, but I could only pronounce the first two words, because at once their cries and sobs began again stronger than before throughout the chapel. I was obliged to abstain a second time to the ferocity of their grief. The fruit of all this was that they no longer talked of anything but of having been converted and giving themselves entirely to God.

The same day, the next, and for the following eight days, excessive penances were performed at the Sault. It would have been difficult for more to be done from the most austere penitents in the world. The devotion became general and all the Natives spoke of penance, self-denial, renouncing all so as to give all to God in imitation of Catherine. In truth, they came from every side to inform me of these beautiful and holy resolutions and what was more, they had succeeded in accomplishing them.

A woman had passed the night of Good Friday rolling herself on thorns as Catherine had done. A little later, another did this for four or five consecutive nights, and married people separated so as to live in continence and widows renounced a second marriage. The younger women promised they would renounce a second marriage if their husbands were the first to die. And so ardent was the zeal for bodily penance in the mission, that I truly risk saying that the most rigid monasteries never came to such terrifying mortification that these new converts voluntarily imposed upon themselves. In time, they have done these holy resolutions and persevered in them.

The men and women had covered themselves with blood from disciplinary stripes in imitation of Catherine. They fasted rigorously and would pass the entire days without eating. What the Natives would eat during half of the year would not have been sufficient to keep a man alive. These were the great fruits produced by the life and death of Catherine Tekakwitha at the Mission of the Sault. The memory of this generous virgin is carefully preserved there and through the care of the missionaries, who often remind her virtues to the Natives.

The women mixed ashes in their portions of sagamite, placed glowing coals between their toes, went barelegged to make a long procession in the snow and disfigured themselves by cutting their hair because they did not want to be sought in marriage. There were Native girls who threw themselves in the water during the middle of the winter. These austerities were almost continual and inflicted all the harm they could do to the body, because they say it is their greatest enemy. Most of these austerities took place in the forest. The Holy Spirit would, however, soon intervene in this matter. It had enlightened them and regulated their conduct without lessening their fervour.

Chapter 17

After having spoken until now of her life and death, we shall consider some apparitions of Catherine. Also, of the extraordinary favours several people had obtained from heaven, and are being received everyday in New France. I will admit with regard to these apparitions that I had difficulty deciding whether to speak of it, because there are too many people in the world making themselves believe nothing, especially in matters of this sort. They would no sooner hear of her apparitions mentioned that they protest against them and pretend these revelations are many illusions. These people would prefer to believe that the hand of God was shortened concerning the apparitions of a poor Native girl, but He is the giver of all the graces and would give them to anyone He wants.

The appearances I am referring to here are such of an importance and clear in detail. I do not see that they could reasonably be doubted. The incredulous will always remain so. God will be glorified in His servant and virtuous people will find in these marvels new motives to love and bless Him, seeing how He rewards the services rendered to Him and even from the poor Natives.

On the sixth day after Catherine's death; that is to say, the Monday after Easter, Father Chauchetiere was praying at four o'clock in the morning when Catherine appeared to him. She was surrounded by glory, with full majestic bearing and her shining face lifted to heaven as if in ecstasy. He saw Catherine all in white as a rising sun and heard these words, "Adhunc veni in dies" that is to say, "Even now I come everyday." This marvellous apparition was accompanied with three circumstances that had rendered it more admirable.

In the first place, the appearance had lasted two entire hours. The Father could contemplate her at leisure as a portrait. He did with such a joy and pleasure that it is difficult to express. Catherine wanted from this appearance to recognize the favour of his great services received from him during her lifetime. This same apparition was accompanied with several prophecies and from as many symbols seen on the two sides of Catherine in her ecstasy.

In the apparition, he saw at the right of Catherine a chapel turned over on its side and while at her left that a Native was tied to a stake and burned alive. These events occurred in August of 1683, and then in the year, 1690. The Father wanted to have kept this appearance as a secret. In truth, he did not actually disclose it until a much later time, which was when the events seen as symbols took place and Catherine began to be famous for her miracles.

At midnight, which was the joining of the night of Thursday, the nineteenth to Friday, the twentieth of August,

1683 that there was a terrible storm with such lightning, thunder and the earth was seen to tremble. An evil spirit could only have caused such a storm. It hurled the chapel of the Sault and breaking it into pieces. I say it had taken the chapel with such violence at one corner that it was turned over on the opposite angle. All the articles of the sacred furniture were preserved entirely, except five crosses that were broken and that may represent the faith of the five nations. The statue of the Blessed Virgin had simply overturned and was at an elevation of eleven feet.

Above the inside of the chapel, there were two Jesuit Fathers. Fathers Jean Morain and Nicolas Jean Potier. They were lifted into the air with the pieces. Father Chauchetiere came from the cabin and went inside the chapel to ring the bell to alert the village of the storm. He felt the rope pulled out of his hands and was lifted as the others. He was saved and carried away from the place where he had been kneeling and at his feet the two bells fell. Also, a great hole in the ground was made near him from the joists, which were broken in their fall. He found himself in a place of safety without fear and wounded. He prayed and kissed Catherine's relics that he had tied around his neck. Father Potier leaped into the air with the rafters, which had formed a sort of cage around him and escaped with a slight wound to his face. Father Morain fell and had his shoulder dislocated, but soon recovered. All the three Fathers had found themselves on the ground under the debris. They were rescued with much difficulty.

The Fathers thought their bodies could have been severely injured from such a violent situation, but merely received some slight wounds. They had attributed being alive to the prayers said to Catherine and when all three of the

Fathers met, one of them said, "As for me that I had said mass of the Holy Trinity as in honour of Catherine this morning." The other said, "I went to her grave this morning as to recommend myself to her in a very particular manner." And Father Chauchetiere said, "For over a year that I had an insistent idea of an accident would happen to the mission and during all that time, and even today, I went to pray to Catherine at her grave to deliver us from it. And besides this, I did not cease to importune the Superior of the mission to have her bones placed in our chapel."

Father Chauchetiere could not restrain his tears when he saw the Natives, who were so afflicted by the loss of their chapel. They said that God was chasing them away from the chapel, because they did not deserve to enter it. They were inconsolable at seeing these Fathers wounded and sick. They said that these Fathers were suffering for them, because they were not willing to listen and live like good Christians. He was very skilful and took the opportunity to encourage them to change their lives in earnest.

Then God, having placed in the village an architect who built five other chapels very well constructed. They immediately proceeded to rebuild the chapel. The senior and most fervent of the Chiefs of the Sault, the Great Macqua, finished his bark cabin fifteen days ago. He left his cabin because he offered it to serve as a chapel until another was built. The offer of the Great Macqua was accepted and he considers himself the happiest man in his village because he had the blessedness of giving lodging to Jesus Christ. Our Lord had honoured this chapel with several wonders that occurred therein, where many people said novenas to Catherine Tekakwitha because they were seen to come to the chapel from devotion. They performed the same devotion there regardless of the severities of winter, the spring rains or the summer heat, which was harder to endure for those that often went to visit the Blessed Sacrament.

The Native seen burnt at the stake in the apparition, although he died a glorious death, would happen in 1690 at Onondaga. He was Stephan Teganannokoa and he was a Huron from the Mission of Saint Francis Xavier. When in the midst of the flames, he did not cease to encourage his wife to invoke with him the Holy Name of Jesus. Having been near death, he revived all his strength and in imitation of Jesus Christ, he prayed to Him with a loud voice for the conversion of those who treated him with such inhumanity.

In the two following years at Onondaga, two Onondaga women of the Mission of Saint Francis Xavier, Frances Gonannhatenha and Margaret Garangouas, were also captured and burned out of hatred for the faith and the mission.

The French, who were slaves among the Iroquois, were continually escaping. They were witnesses, so they could not relate these things to us without weeping and drawing tears from the eyes of their listeners. Catherine had prophesied this a long time before and obtained of these Natives the invincible courage that they had during their torture. We shall regard this at the end of this book, and was the marvellous result of the influence she has in heaven.

In the following year, Monday the first of September, 1681, and on Tuesday the twenty-first of April 1682, Catherine appeared again to Father Chauchetiere. The Father was left in contemplation for five entire hours after the apparition on Monday September 1, 1681. Then he again was left in contemplation, but for six entire hours after the apparition on Tuesday April 21, 1682. These two appearances of her were under the same circumstances as to the first. The only difference was that these two apparitions that he had seen her as the sun at noon in mid-heaven; that is to say, as a very brilliant white light.

In the first of the last two apparitions, Catherine Tekakwitha appeared to the Father while shining with brilliant lustre in all her person. The Father had felt an interior inspiration to show her painted image to the people.

In the last apparition he had of Catherine, the Father saw Catherine Tekakwitha so brilliant with surrounding light, and this time his eyes could scarcely endure seeing her. Also, he heard these words, "Inspice et fac secundum exemplar" that is to say, "See that you make them according to the pattern" (Exodus 25:40). God had made it known that He wanted portraits to be painted of Catherine. Now he was demanded to paint a portrait of her as he saw her. He made the painting and it was as the best that he could. Later, other paintings were done by Father Chauchetiere, but were badly done on paper, although the people value them so much. There are scarcely enough to supply the requests for these paintings, and people are very grateful to these paintings and they carefully have kept them in their cabins. The Father had for a long time refrained from painting portraits of Catherine, but when he painted portraits of her later on, they contributed a great deal to making Catherine known, because they were placed on the heads of the sick and they brought about marvellous cures.

Two days after the first of these apparitions, Wednesday April 24, 1680, Catherine appeared to the good Anastasia in the following manner. She said, "One night after the public prayers and when everyone had gone to sleep, I had prayed alone a little while and then I went also to sleep. I scarcely had fallen asleep when I was awakened from a voice calling me and saying, 'My mother, rise up and look!' I had recognized Catherine's voice. Immediately, I sat up and turning to the side of the place, where she was calling me. I had seen her standing at my side. She had half of her body hidden until the belt. Her upper body was of a brilliant white light and I saw only her face that was of extraordinary beauty. She said, 'My mother, look well at the cross I am carrying! Look, look, how beautiful the cross is! Ah, how I loved the cross on earth! Ah, how I love the cross still in paradise! How much I want all of our cabin to love and rely on the cross as I did!' This was what she had said to me and at that instant, she disappeared and left me with so full of joy. And the cross she carried in her hand was so beautiful and gave forth more brilliant light than all the rest; I have never seen anything so lovely and charming." Her spirit was so filled with this apparition that after many years her memory is still as fresh as the first day.

Through this loving visit, it would seem that Catherine wanted to show her gratefulness of all the care that she had from Anastasia, because she looked at her as her mother. Catherine had wanted from her words and from the apparition of this beautiful cross to prepare the cross generously, because God wanted to prepare her for the death of three of her children in wars. The oldest of them was one of the Chiefs of the village. These great sufferings she endured with heroic faithfulness and she was greatly strengthened from this apparition of her dear daughter.

The great affection Catherine had to the cross and the manner she appeared to her mother gave the thought of painting her with a cross in her hand. It was the posture that was the most appropriate for her. The cross was the source of all her happiness during her life.

Chapter 18

God had spoken even more visibly on the sanctity and the merit of Catherine, who is His spouse from authentic testimonies. These testimonies are the tremendous graces, a great number of which have been granted and are continuing to be granted through her intercession. It is time that we should speak of one of the most beautiful places of her history. It will give a new lustre to the rest of her history.

I already said in the beginning that we had at the mission such a rich treasure in Catherine. However, we kept this truth hidden from our village judging it prudent not to precipitate matters. It was to wait until heaven had given a sign to make her known. This sign occurred through a movement that could have come from God alone.

After her death, the Natives frequented Catherine's grave. They went to pray and began to visit her on the very day that she was buried. The Natives and the French were alike in their zeal to honour her and to recommend themselves to her prayers. Several of them had received interior graces for the good of their souls. The knowledge of Catherine had spread from the cure of the souls, which is more important than that of the bodies. These cures happened soon after her death. After nine months from her burial, bodily healings were to begin.

While at the time, Father Chauchetiere had felt strongly inspired to publish Catherine's virtues, this would have made her known to the world. At these moments he went as far as to disapprove in his soul the honours given to Catherine at her grave. Although at other times, he was so moved by her virtues that he went to her grave and honoured her more than anyone else.

In January 1681, a year after Catherine's death, someone sought Father Chauchetiere at the Sault. I want to describe it here at length for the glory of Catherine. This is to show through what method God began to make known the merit and the influence of His servant. Apart from the mission, the Father had served the spiritual needs of the French at La Prairie de la Madeleine and was asked to assist Claude Caron, who was dying. The Father felt an extreme joy from the bottom of his heart, believing that he would find the means that he sought for a long time to enlighten himself concerning this Iroquois virgin and prove if she was as powerful in heaven.

He went to see the sick man, but only after having been to Catherine's grave. At her grave, he prayed on his knees and begged Jesus Christ to enlighten him in this matter as to settle his doubts. During his prayer, he felt an increasing joy and together with an assured confidence Catherine was able to cure this sick man. The Father had found the man dying from a violent chest pain after a third relapse and heard his last Confession, but this man could scarcely speak. The Father gave him Holy Communion and exhorted him to take courage with confidence in God that he might then recover. The Father told of the thought of placing him under Catherine's protection.

The sick man had willingly agreed. Immediately he promised, if he was cured, he would go to the Sault and thank her at her grave. The Father gave him the crucifix that Catherine's hands held when she was buried and left him with the promise to return the following morning. Before having left, the Father had him recite an Our Father, a Hail Mary and three times the Glory Be to the Father. Also, the Father had the sick man promise to say three masses in thanksgiving to God for the graces conferred to Catherine.

A moment later, they wanted to take him from the place where he was lying so they could readjust it, but he fell on the floor like a man about to die. All they could do was to place him quickly back where he was lying so that he could at least die more easily, but the contrary happened. When he lay down, he was caught by a light sleep; and during his light sleep, he felt as if a great stone were removed from his chest. When he awoke, he was cured and entirely out of danger. He even ate with appetite and slept peacefully during the following night.

Before the arrival of the Father, a surgeon from Montreal had come to see the man and then departed to obtain a remedy, but more to the good of having pleased the man, because the surgeon had no hope of curing him. When he had returned with the medicine the following morning, the day after the Father left, he was greatly astonished to see the man completely cured and sitting next to the fire, eating. A great weakness was the only remaining sign of his illness. He had recovered later through nourishment and rest. The surgeon declared that he had never seen a sick man who did not die from this disease.

Father Chauchetiere was not able to come to see him until three or four days later. He then had the pleasure of finding the man in perfect health and the Father was told all of what happened. After the cured man recovered, he fulfilled his promise to visit Catherine's grave and to thank his benefactress. This was the first bodily cure that was done by Catherine.

I shall now relate a second cure, which took place at the very village of La Prairie and this cure was all the more remarkable, because it was accompanied by many graces and witnessed from all the inhabitants of the village. It was likewise in the month of January 1681, some time after the preceding cure. The wife of Francis Rouanais fell seriously ill and was soon at the point of death.

She received all the Last Sacraments from the same Father who gave her the crucifix that had served at the first cure and exhorted her to recommend herself to Catherine with confidence in her power. She had Catherine's crucifix tied around her neck and as soon as this was done, in the presence of her children, she was instantly cured. She believed that the crucifix cured her, but she had great difficulty in persuading herself to leave the crucifix. She could not decide to do so until the Father gave her a little of the earth from Catherine's grave. She placed this earth in a small cloth bag and tied around her neck instead of the crucifix. Some time later, feeling completely cured, she removed the earth and at this very moment she became sick and thought she would die. Then someone quickly replaced this earth around her neck and suddenly that she was healed. This miraculous earth would do so many marvels and was the same that obtained the cure on the first occasion for her, but the miracle did not end there. This virtuous and wise woman has always carried the relic on her for the gratitude to Catherine, who had twice cured her and who feared to become ill a third time if she were to remove it.

A year later, she became ill again. Her husband had a violent pain in his back from rheumatism. When his wife saw seen him in this condition, she took the dust relic from her neck and tied it around the neck of her husband. He was instantly cured, but the pain had passed over to his wife, who began to cry out loud saying that her husband was killing her. It was necessary to take the dust away from her husband, who had been healed from it on the instant to return it to his wife. She was cured a third time as soon as she had tied it around her neck. They lived in good health for a long time after this. All this was marvellous before the eyes of all the inhabitants of La Prairie de la Madeleine.

In March 1682, the power of Catherine began to be felt at the Sault, where sixty cabins or one hundred twenty to one hundred and fifty families lived. A Christian Iroquois, who had received the Last Sacraments and whose death was expected, had the same Father take some of the earth from Catherine's grave. Again, someone had escaped death and regained his health. This man spent five years in fighting a vice, but he promised Catherine to rid himself before he was cured. After his cure, he fulfilled his promise. When the Father saw that the man was out of danger, he told us what had been done.

Then I named a young woman crippled in all her limbs from the age of eight or nine years old that could not move her hands and feet. She was afflicted every spring and was not able to find a successful remedy. She also had the name Catherine and was devotedly attached to Catherine Tekakwitha when she was living.

The Father went to the cabin of this woman and the condition that he found her in made him compassionate towards her sufferings. He pressed her to have recourse to Catherine Tekakwitha. He gave Catherine's crucifix to wear around her neck and began a novena in her honour. During the novena, she should say everyday an Our Father, a Hail Mary and three times the Glory Be to the Father. This was the first novena said to Catherine Tekakwitha.

On the ninth day, the woman was cured and for fourteen years now she has been without her sickness. The Father had told her to remember the promise that she made to Catherine Tekakwitha; that is, not to gamble any more. She would never gamble from the day she was cured. This woman had scarcely been restored to health when her husband, who was the oldest son of the good Anastasia, became a victim of the same sickness.

In the month of April, Catherine cured him and after her aid was invoked. She kept him from a death where he might have been taken to heaven, but she wanted to deliver him later from despair that nearly sent him to hell. A few days after his cure, he had an argument with his mother. He abruptly left and ran along the road on the side of the Great River to throw himself into it. He was fortunate to pass near and opposite to Catherine's grave, where he suddenly lost the ability to move his legs. He stood there, having only the feelings of his legs, until he realized his sin and asked forgiveness from God for his sin. He went to confess forthwith and declared what had happened to the glory of Catherine. It has been known that Catherine usually cured the souls of the people who's bodies she had healed even though they did not pray for it, but were in need of this cure.

The following summer in 1682, Mary Garhi was pregnant and came into labour while in the fields. She was the wife of Hot Ashes, who was the principal Chief at the Sault. She was carried to her cabin in a dying condition. The women and a French midwife could not relieve her suffering. Our Lord wanted to have her be under Catherine's obligation. In truth, the woman was pressed to commend herself to Catherine.

They brought Catherine's blanket, which was in the custody of her companion. The bell was rung for the morning mass and everyone went to pray for Mary Garhi, who remained alone. Then she took the blanket with full confidence and threw the blanket over her body and with a prayer to Catherine to have pity on her. While praying, she placed her hand on the blanket, over the abdomen, and was cured at once. When the women returned to the cabin after the mass, to their astonishment they found her relieved of her trouble. This they perceived as a new sense of the influence and merit of Catherine.

All these miraculous cures made Catherine's name famous. The people began to have masses and novenas said in her honour. We have now seen many people going to pray at her grave. The cures became so numerous that we ceased to mark them. In truth, every month or every week of this year would pass and great miracles occurred at the Sault and in the French settlements. However, it was known for several years that Catherine had limited herself to the country and to the poor people. She had wanted first to gratify the Sault, where her body is buried and then to La Prairie and the Mission of Lachine, which are the two French settlements nearest to the source and entrance of the river. The healing power that would emanate from her grave began with joy and soon spread beyond the village into the surrounding settlements.

In October 1683, I found in the history of the miracles Catherine brought during my absence from the Sault, in which Father Jean Morain was cured of paralysis during a novena he said to Catherine.

One of our Fathers had come back entirely paralysed from the province of Guiana and recommended himself to her. He promised God when returning to the islands that he would work with great zeal for the salvation of their souls. He was cured and returned to the islands, and from there he wrote to us about this miracle and begged us to thank her for him at the Sault.

When Rene Cuillerier was living at his fort and near the Mission of Lachine, he heard of Catherine and of the miracles that she brought about when he was at La Prairie for his work. He was the first to introduce devotion to her in Lachine. A little later, his wife Marie was in extraordinary pain at childbirth and recommended herself to Catherine. She had promised to thank her at her grave if she gave birth to her child safely. Then the woman went into a gentle sleep and during it she delivered without pain. She did not wake until the baby cried out. She said to her husband, "I had promised to make a pilgrimage to her grave." The two became aware that they made the same promise without communicating to each other of their thoughts. Some time later, they came to thank Catherine, who had heard their prayers. This event made Catherine known at the Mission of Lachine. She made many and such astonishing miraculous cures there that she became known with the name of the Good Catherine. This is what the good people have always called her.

Two years later, one of his children was cured by the invocation of this virtuous girl. His wife had taken the child to the Chapel of Saint Francis Xavier at the Sault, where the bones of Catherine Tekakwitha rest. They had placed him on her tomb, a mass was said there and a novena was said to obtain from God the cure of her son through the merits of His servant. As soon as the novena was completely said, the child began to feel better and from then on he lived in perfect health.

In 1680, Father Pierre Remy was appointed Pastor at Lachine. However, he had doubts about the cures reported as obtained through a Native girl. But after the Pastor himself had obtained certain favours, he himself, promoted a great devotion for her.

In 1687, Jeanne Merein lived in his Parish and came to ask him to say a mass in thanksgiving for a cure, which she received from God from the intercession of Catherine Tekakwitha. She was the wife of Rene le Moreau who had been also cured by this saint from some trouble. Father Remy had been afflicted with deafness in his right ear and completely prevented him absolutely from hearing confessions on that side. While he was preparing to say this mass, an urgent thought came to him to invoke this good young girl, Catherine, to cure of his deafness. After the Communion of this mass, he suddenly felt that his hearing had improved and when the mass was over the deafness ceased. From that day on, he had perfect and complete confidence in this holy young woman.

He fulfilled his vow the following days of offering three masses. After this, he proclaimed her as a saint everywhere.

CATHERINE TEKAKWITHA: BOOK TWO

We had the pleasure last year of seeing him come two times to say mass here at the mission to thank God for the grace given to Catherine and the several years of her graces rendered to him and his parishioners. So great were these miracles that he said to us that in his Parish there were not many sick people because the earth from Catherine's grave had been a prompt and an assured remedy against all sorts of diseases.

He allowed his parishioners to come here two consecutive years in 1694 and 1695 to have High Mass sung with the best bread and many communions in honour of their benefactress. In 1696, the seventeenth of April was the Tuesday of Holy Week and the anniversary of Catherine's death. He had come with his parishioners for the same devotions. He received other graces from God through the intercession of Catherine Tekakwitha, which have to do with his spiritual and his temporal needs.

The Commandant of Fort Lachine Francis Guantier de Rane and his wife had made a pilgrimage and presented their donation of the consecrated bread to thank Catherine because she had previously cured him from continuous vomiting. He was cured after having the Father say a novena to Catherine and three masses at the mission for his intention. During that time, the Father had him take water in which a small cloth bag with the ashes of Catherine's clothing was soaked. They came that day to fulfill their promise together with their Pastor, who was Father Remy, and with others. It should do so much for the glory of Catherine, because having come from a person of such merit and of recognized virtue in New France.

In January 1684, a child of three years old was choking on a shell and when her mother had dedicated her to Catherine the child was saved.

Another child, who was very sick, had been completely cured after her mother placed on her head a small painting of Catherine, which she was able to obtain. Then the girl ran along the road at the side of the river and they lost sight of her for some time.

A third woman had spoken in derision at those that advised her to devote herself to Catherine for her sick child. This woman ridiculed all that was said in honour of Catherine. She was punished immediately, because the illness became worst. When she had realized her fault, she invoked Catherine and the child recovered soon after.

I have excluded here a large number of similar cures at Montreal, Pointe-aux-Trembles, Boucherville, Saint-Lambert, La Prairie de la Madeleine and other places, so as to recount only the most important cures that occurred more recently.

In 1684, many of the Natives were in such a necessity to offered their devotion to the deceased Catherine Tekakwitha. They believed that it was a tribute merited to her virtue. She was removed from the cemetery, where a little monument had been placed to her a year before in 1683. With all the opinions sharing the same sentiments, they brought her into the new chapel they had just finished building at the Sault. This transfer was accomplished during the night and was in the presence of the most devout persons and Father Chauchetiere, who was then the Superior of the mission.

Her grave had been surrounded with some children who died between her burial and January 1681. This was before we began to see whether Catherine was influential in heaven to intercede for bodily cures.

CATHERINE TEKAKWITHA: BOOK TWO

The beginning of 1689, the village was transferred by the Governor to Montreal until early 1690. The Natives from the Sault had remained among the French in Montreal. The mission returned to the Sault, but a few leagues higher, where the missionaries founded Kahnawakon. In 1695, the missionaries again transferred the mission. They then had founded Kanatawenke, where we are presently. The relics of Catherine followed with them in all their displacements.

We received word from Quebec that Father Jacques Fremin died on Friday July 20, 1691, from a great sickness. We do not know whether he invoked Catherine's intercession.

In the winter of 1693, Father Bruyas was still in charge of the mission. He was suddenly seized with paralysis of the right arm and was not able to move it. Immediately, he was taken to Montreal to be cured of his trouble. Before he departed, he asked all those that were members of the small society of the Sisters of Catherine to begin a novena to Catherine. This society is still called Catherine's Band at the mission. The novena was begun on a Thursday morning. Although he was in Montreal, he did not decide to take the remedies because he had great confidence in Catherine's power to cure him. He had continued saying this until the following Thursday and even though it was the eighth day of the novena, there was no change in the condition of his arm. In truth, Catherine was concerned over the health of Father Chauchetiere, who had actually the charge of her own dear mission, but she did not fail to cure Father Bruyas. On Friday, the last day of the novena, the Father awoke at four o'clock in the morning and found his arm healed. He was able to say mass, which he had not been able to do for eight days and thus gave thanks to Our Lord and Catherine.

Diego Paoletti

A young woman from Onondaga, the sister of Margaret Gagouithon, was living at the village of Kahnawakon and had gone on the hunt with her husband in the winter of 1694. She was pregnant when she had left and reached her time in the early spring. It would seem that the Native women have not inherited the curse of Eve, because with such an ease do they give birth. They accomplished deliveries in the fields, forest or during a voyage; and after having given birth; they would work in the forest or carry on their everyday work of the cabin. However, this was not the situation of this particular woman.

Her labour lasted three days and three nights without delivery, and in the midst of such terrifying pains she became almost despaired. At the very end, she thought of Catherine. At once, in the midst of her pain, she said devotedly to Catherine these few words that I will leave you to judge whether they were from the depths of her heart, "Catherine have pity on me! Obtain delivery of me soon and if mine shall be a girl, I will promise she shall have your name." At that moment, she went into a calm sleep and she delivered even more calmly. She was later awaken by the crying of her baby. The baby was a girl, who she brought her to the village and asked me to baptize her as Catherine. Then she told me of the entire thing.

We have come to the year 1695. It was a beautiful year for Catherine and the one in which it seems God wanted to make her triumph in New France. Her triumph came from the extraordinary miracles that she did for the most prominent people.

In February 1695 and in the island of Montreal, Our Lord wanted to have appeared a great miracle and had shone forth this throughout New France. This was the cure of the wife of

CATHERINE TEKAKWITHA: BOOK TWO

Alphonse de Tonti. He was the brother of Henri de Tonti and an officer of Commandant Antoine Laumet. They thought she would die, so she received all the Last Sacraments and they said to her the Recommendations of the Soul. Father Chauchetiere was sent to have him hear her Confession. After her Confession, the Father had her take some earth from Catherine's grave. Suddenly, she was cured in the presence of Father Francis Dollier de Casson, who was the Superior of the Society of the Priests of the Seminary of Saint-Sulpice and also the Grand Vicar of Bishop de Saint-Vallier. Father Chauchetiere said that this cure brought universal consent of everyone that we could all honour a Native as a saint. After this, many others would come nearly every day to him for earth from Catherine's grave.

It was already more than two years since the Intendant Jean Bochart de Champigny began suffering from a heavy cold. At last it became worst and he almost lost his voice. His wife wrote to us in the letter, which we had the honour to receive at the mission, asking us to say a novena to Catherine. We were so much interested in his health with all of New France, that we did all that was possible. The Sisters of Catherine said the novena. Fortunately, they were all present at the village. He was cured of his cold in Quebec during the novena. I do not doubt that on this occasion Catherine wanted to reward the great obligations of all our missions and that of the Mission of Saint Francis Xavier, especially to him and his wife by the notable charities that they have done and still do to us every day.

In New France, everyone would know of the devotion and zeal they have of Catherine Tekakwitha. He and his wife had distributed portraits of her in New France and sent some to France for the important people at the first court of the world. Because of this, God benefited from the piety of so prominent a person to make a poor Native known. God had blessed this action, because we received knowledge from Paris, France, that Catherine had cured a dying person and that is all we know about it now.

In June 1695, the cure of the Indendant gave the occasion to Father Joseph de la Colombiere, Canon of the Cathedral of Quebec, who is well known for his virtue. He was advised to make a vow if God pleased to end his slow fever. He had it for five months accompanied by his dysentery, and all the medications were ineffective. His vow was to go to the Mission of Saint Francis Xavier and pray at the tomb of Catherine Tekakwitha. The fever ceased that same day he took the vow and the dysentery diminished considerably. He left a few days later to keep his promise. Before he made a third of the journey, he was completely cured. We had the pleasure of having him with us for a few days at the mission, where he came to thank his benefactress. He came again in September 1696. On leaving us, he gave large alms to the poor of the mission and wrote an attestation from Montreal on Friday September 14, 1696, for his cure, which is worthy of his piety.

A short time after that he made his first pilgrimage here in the summer, Catherine Foucault had come from Quebec to ask a favour. She had terrible headaches and came to ask Catherine to cure her. She had a mass said at the mission and received Communion. Then she remained for a long time after praying in the middle of the church where the tomb of Catherine Tekakwitha was. During her prayer, she had felt as if something was torn from her head and she suffered considerably, but it then left her completely cured of her trouble.

M. de Granville had spent the summer in Montreal behind the Governor of New France, Louis de Buade Frontenac. The Governor spoke well to him of Catherine and said that he had thought of bringing back to Quebec some earth from Catherine's grave. When he returned to Quebec in the autumn, one of his daughters was dying and she was still very young. Upon seeing him, his wife could not avoid saying, "My husband! My husband! You have come well at the right moment to see your child die." He replied, "No! No! I brought her cure with me." He was speaking of the earth he carried with him. He soaked the little cloth bag of earth in the water that they had the little girl drink. Then they both knelt down and recommended their daughter to Catherine. She recovered immediately. He began to cry, "Miracle! Miracle!" He went to proclaim it throughout the town of Quebec.

A poor orphan girl of the country was tormented by violent hiccoughs and could not find a remedy. She was sent to Fathers Dollier de Casson and de Belmont for some earth from Catherine's grave that she had taken in water and was cured. Father Dollier de Casson sent her the following day to our church and received Holy Communion in thanksgiving of her cure.

Three children of the same town that is, one of the family Boisseau, another of the family Parent and the third whose family I do not know, were all cured of fever after drinking some water from Catherine's cup. There are many other cures similar to these in the island of Montreal. I exclude them here and as not to have tired the reader with a repetition of the same matter. However, I cannot refrain from mentioning the healing of the father of one the children of the family Boisseau we have just mentioned, because it seems to be extraordinary.

It is well known that cancer is a disease and affects every part of the flesh. When it attacks, it does not end until the patient dies after having endured a long and cruel martyrdom. He did not think that this illness was beyond the healing power of Catherine. He began a novena to her and when this had no result, he said a second novena and then without losing hope, a third novena was said. During his third novena, his cancer had begun to disappear and it left him completely cured. He retained only the scar of it.

These were all bodily healings, but Catherine had also brought the cure to souls that are of infinitely greater importance. I know of more than thirty people that Catherine has aided to reform their lives. She also delivered others from temptations of the flesh and obtained them the gift of chastity. In this matter, Catherine had obtained particular graces to the souls of others. Two young women of about fifteen years of age, piously raised girls, had begun to discuss what they could do in imitation of Catherine to please God. They thought nothing would be more pleasing to choose Jesus as their Spouse and to their Mother, Mary, by making a vow of virginity as Catherine had done. They agreed together and commended their plan to God and Catherine in prayer. However, one difficult and perhaps insurmountable obstacle stood in their way. This was that their parents would never consent. With having renewed their love of God and inspired with a fresh desire of preserving their virginity, they began to importune Catherine more earnestly. If they could not remain virgins, they would want to receive the grace of dying as virgins through her intercession. Catherine had heard their prayer and as we could piously believe because not long after, and beyond all expectations, the two girls died. I shall say a few words that are true, that the power of Catherine Tekakwitha would reach to the very soul.

A Sister at Montreal was very sick and suffering from a pain on her side. A Father of the Mission of Saint Francis Xavier sent to her a tooth of Catherine and a plate from she had eaten. The Sister was cured after she placed the tooth in her mouth and drank from the plate.

Joseph Kellogg contracted smallpox and when the sickness was at the height that the sores were white. A Father who was from our mission gave him the rotten wood of Catherine's coffin, which he took with water. After he went to sleep, he had recovered and gained weight. He was reminded of the promise that he made and how angry God would be with him if he would not keep the promise. Soon after, he had fulfilled his promise that was confessing and converting to a Roman Catholic.

I have spoken for a while of the many graces Catherine Tekakwitha had granted throughout New France, but I must not forget those that she gave and continues to give us at the mission. A grace that will be called the greatest of her marvels is the preservation of the mission, which we can attribute only to her prayers and the precious remains that we possess.

We have seen fifteen hundred Iroquois burning the entire border of Lachine. They passed along the length of our territories and near enough to our fields to destroy them if they had wanted, but not a single ear of corn was lost. During the eight years that the war has been raging, they could have come during the sowing season or in the summer throughout the harvest and devastated the mission in Kahnawakon, and even after in Kanatawenke in the spring. They would say every year that it was the last year of the Sault, but the mission still survives. In the three years that I have been here, only one poor old woman was killed during these sowing seasons and harvests.

In the early spring of 1695, one of the renegades had come from the Macquas. He came to search for his mother and sister at the mission. He said that the Iroquois planned for our destruction the following summer and that everyone here must perish. In the summer, the warriors of the village left us to conduct a convoy to Fort Catarakoui and only the old men remained with the women.

Then all summer long, we were moving our village and everyone was carting and carrying from Kahnawakon to Kanatawenke. Not one Iroquois came into sight, even though they knew very well what was happening.

Further on, they rained a shower of bullets upon the five or six approaching canoes, which were filled with more than thirty women. Among them were the most prominent from the mission and the Sisters of Catherine. In this fierce and unexpected attack, one of the oldest and bravest of the women began to recite the Litany of Our Lady. The attackers left without having touched and pierced a single canoe. Several Iroquois had thrown themselves into the water to take hold of the canoes of these women, but without success. These women came to land at the side of the du Portage River, where Catherine's grave was as well as the village of the Sault. This miracle, in all its details, could be explained that it happened within sight of Catherine's grave. Catherine had blinded the enemies. Also, she inspired confidence and readiness among the women so they could be saved from their enemy.

Catherine had inspired courage in another group of women, who were met by some who came from the Macqua lands. The Macquas having themselves seen that they came upon this other group of women were of their own relations and wanted to take these women with them. It was unbelievable for the Macquas to prevail upon them. The women had protested that they would rather die than to abandon their faith and the men could kill them as their slaves. This greatly astonished the raiders, who had not wanted to avenge themselves on the women, but they decided to bring them to the mission and to make a truce with these women and the others of the village.

When the villages of Onondaga and Oneida were burned, more than ever that they could have come to avenge us during the harvest, but we harvested in perfect security. All the warriors from the village had gone to the territory of the Macquas and the English. The women were in the fields from morning to evening with their children at half a league from the village. Some even slept in the fields as in the time of peace and not one of our enemies appeared. We had regarded these things as one of the many marvels of our Guardian Angel, our powerful protectress and patroness, the brave Catherine Tekakwitha. She has for a long time preserved her beloved mission. We hope that she will continue to preserve and augment it more our present mission at Kanatawenke, which is from the opposition of our enemies whether they are visible or invisible.

Heaven grants a great many favours to those who beseech her intercession, and Ecclesiastics and laymen come to this mission on pilgrimage to thank God for the favours they have received through her intercession. Presents are sent to the church where her body lies to show their gratitude to their benefactress in thanksgiving to God. Entire parishes come to the church in solemn procession on the anniversary of the death of Catherine Tekakwitha to give thanks of the various favours received from her protection. All the French in the colonies and the Natives have an exceptional veneration for Catherine. They speak of her everywhere with praise and they invoke her name. The Natives regard her as a powerful patroness given to them from God for the preservation of their country against their enemies.

In March 1696, Father Remy wrote to me three letters of legal attestations for the many miraculous cures done from the intercession of Catherine Tekakwitha at his Mission of Holy Angels in Lachine. He was a witness to all the cures and they were all done from the same earth or the ashes from her clothing, which he had all his sick take. He would have them say nine prayers of the Hail Mary a day for every day of the novena and he would consecrate them to God at holy mass during the same nine days, which were through the hands and intercession of Catherine Tekakwitha.

In March of the same year, Joseph-Daniel Greysolon du Luth, who is a Captain in the Marine Corps and Commandant at Fort Catarakoui, was cured from his gout on the ninth day of the novena that he had said to Catherine. He gave an attestation on Wednesday August 15, 1696, for his cure. Then he came to the mission this summer because of the promise he made to visit her tomb if God should give him health through her intercession.

The wife of Jean Bochart de Champigny has scarcely passed a year without coming to the mission for the purpose of honouring Catherine and having prayed in our church at the foot of her relics.

The French from every part of the colony comes to this place to give thanks of the favours received from Catherine and venerate her relics that are kept in our church.

On Friday September 21, 1696, the feast of Saint Matthew, more than twenty distinguished people came from Montreal came to satisfy their devotion at our church in

Kanatawenke. They wanted to ask favours from Catherine or to return their thanks for the favours that they had already obtained. A still greater had come over the ice during the winter.

Catherine's mere paintings, just the invocation of her name, only the promise of a pilgrimage to her relics, water drank from her cup, her clothing or ashes from her clothing and the touching of anything she had touched, are all efficacious for curing people that are suffering from any sort of disease. Furthermore, letters from France have told of her aid to many there that besought her.

Father Louis Geoffroy has attested to several very important miracles done by Catherine from his Parish of La Prairie.

In a word, everywhere we missionaries of Kanatawenke go, we hear only of Catherine Tekakwitha, the miracles she performs, the pilgrimages to her tomb to be undertaken, and the masses and novenas said in her honour. God did not hesitate to honour the memory of this virtuous girl. A seemingly infinite number of miraculous cures have taken place after her death and are still continuing everyday through her intercession. There are always pressing demands for a history of her life. It was this that finally had me to make a last effort to satisfy the people in this regard. This I was able to do for the glory of God and of this first Iroquois virgin of Our Lord. At length, I will refrain from writing more.

If I were to write of the many miracles that have been done and are still coming to us from all sides about Catherine Tekakwitha, who died in odour of sanctity, I would go on endlessly and many volumes would be necessary. I shall say this, among the miracles seen as having been rendered through Catherine Tekakwitha, I consider the greatest of them all to be Catherine Tekakwitha herself, as she is truly the Wonder Worker of the New World.

References

Chauchetière, Claude, La vie de la Bonne Catherine Tegakouita, dite à présent la Sainte Sauvagesse, 1695

Chauchetière, Claude, Narration de la mission du Sault depuis sa fondation jusqu'en 1685, 1686

Chauchetière, Claude, lettre du 4 octobre, 1684

Chauchetière, Claude, lettre du 7 août, 1694

Chauchetière, Claude, lettre du 20 septembre, 1694

Chauchetière, Claude, lettre août 1695

Chauchetière, Claude, Recueil de ce qui s'est passé depuis le décès de Catherine, 1684

Cholenec, Pierre, La vie de Catherine Tegakouita, première vierge iroquoise, 1696

Cholenec, Pierre, Abrégé de la vie de Catherine Tegakouita, chrétienne iroquoise, 1696

Cholenec, Pierre, lettre de février, 1680

Cholenec, Pierre, lettre mai 1680

Cholenec, Pierre, lettre écrite en 1718

Cholenec, Pierre, lettre écrite en 1691

Cholenec, Pierre, lettre d'août 1715

Cholenec, Pierre, lettre du 26 septembre 1715

Cholenec, Pierre, lettre du 15 janvier 1678

Cuoq, André, Lexique de la langue iroquoise, 1882

Marcoux, Joseph, Dictionnaire iroquois, 1853